Historic
BLACK SETTLEMENTS
of OHIO

The son of a Randolph slave, Albert McKnight was Piqua's unofficial ambassador. *Piqua Public Library.*

Historic BLACK SETTLEMENTS *of* OHIO

DAVID MEYERS *and* ELISE MEYERS WALKER

THE
History
PRESS

Published by The History Press
Charleston, SC
www.historypress.com

First published 2020

Manufactured in the United States

ISBN 9781467144186

Library of Congress Control Number: 2019951978

Notice: The information in this book is true and complete to the best of our knowledge. It is offered without guarantee on the part of the authors or The History Press. The authors and The History Press disclaim all liability in connection with the use of this book.

To Frank McCray, Edie Wade, Arnett Howard, Karlton Wilson and Melissa Lamar.

CONTENTS

CONTENTS

ACKNOWLEDGEMENTS

Thanks to Sharon R. Watson and Gary Meek of the Piqua Public Library Archives and Special Collections, Randy and Cheryl McNutt, Joyce L. Allig, Dr. Allen Bernard, Jean Miller and Jim Bowsher for their assistance.

INTRODUCTION

I hate the word black; we are not black. My dad would spread his five fingers and tell me to look at his hand. He said that I was like that, a mixture of five bloods—English, Irish, Dutch, Indian and a little bit Negro.
—Doris Bowles Venerable, former Carthagena resident

This is the most challenging book we've ever undertaken. In it, we have attempted to write the story of more than forty vanished communities that were occupied by people of color during a period of our history when they weren't even fully recognized as people. These "Negro" settlements, or colonies, as they were often called, were primarily agrarian and generally located in isolated regions. For the most part, they left no records, and archaeological relics are few, save for scattered cemeteries and a handful of buildings. By the early years of the twentieth century, most of the surviving communities had lost their African American identities.

The residents of these settlements were often emancipated or runaway slaves or, more properly, "enslaved people." We understand and appreciate the distinction that the term "slave" is a passive noun that robs the individual of his or her humanity. It was not who or what they were, but a condition imposed on them by someone else. However, because of our need to repeatedly refer to those who were enslaved, you will find that we also use other terms such as "slave" and "former slave" with no offense intended.

Isaac & Rosa, Slave Children from New Orleans.
PHOTOGRAPHED BY KIMBALL, 477 BROADWAY, N. Y.
Ent'd accord'g to act of Congress in the year 1863, by GEO. H.
HANKS, in the Clerk's Office of the U.S for the So. Dist. of N. Y.

Former slaves Isaac and Rosa exemplified the absurdity of the "one-drop" rule. *Library of Congress.*

The real elephant in the room, though, is how to refer to the race of the individuals. As we have noted in previous books, scientists tend to agree that race is a social construct. *Scientific American* has asserted, "Racial categories are weak proxies for genetic diversity and need to be phased out."[1] Yet American history is primarily the story of racial division—of white and nonwhite—and it cannot be ignored in the telling. We have, therefore, used the terms black or African American and occasionally "colored," "N/ negro," "mulatto," but always when quoting from contemporary sources.

Throughout the book, we have attempted to identify the most common surnames used by the settlers. Researchers have suggested that 15 to 20 percent of former slaves adopted their most recent master's family name; however, the practice varied widely. For example, some 383 former Randolph slaves were brought to Ohio in 1846, yet the Randolph surname was fairly rare among African Americans. Similarly, Virginian Richard Carter freed 485 slaves in 1791, yet not one Carter descendant had been traced back to this event two hundred years later.

As many as half may have chosen names that were not common among the white population as a whole. Furthermore, as Arthur Thomas has pointed out, "Even after a name was chosen, it was often recorded differently at various times due to the low level of literacy and variations in spelling."[2] Goins, Goings, Goens, Goyne and so on are all variations of the same surname. And there are hundreds more.

We suspect that most readers of this book will be surprised to learn that so many black communities were established in Ohio prior to the Civil War. When we set out, we did not know how many there were and still can't say with certainty, but there were more than the ones we have mentioned. The good news is that the conditions that gave rise to these settlements changed. However, we can still see their legacy in the many black neighborhoods that continue to exist in towns and cities throughout the state and the nation. In many respects, we remain a country divided by color.

THE RANDOLPH SLAVES

*O*wing to a common border with the slave states of [West] Virginia and Kentucky, Ohio became a destination for people of color seeking to separate themselves from slavery. Others were brought to the state by their owners and set free. "Ohio officials," historian Stephen Middleton wrote, "charged slave owners with using the state as a 'dumping-ground' for diseased and disabled blacks who were no longer productive."[3] In response, the Ohio General Assembly passed various "Black Laws," which were intended to discourage free blacks, not to mention fugitive slaves, from coming to the state or remaining for long.

They were not the first—nor would they be the last—but the Randolph slaves were the most problematic group of formerly enslaved people to settle in Ohio. And the treatment they were accorded reflected both the best and the worst qualities of the state's citizenry.

Ohio was a free state, but only marginally. There were many supporters of slavery living within its bounds, but even those who were opposed to the institution did not necessarily welcome black refugees. An article published by the *Columbus Free Press* in July 1846 trumpeted, "Great excitement in Mercer County—the importers of the slaves compelled by the people to reship them."[4] The writer then editorialized, "Slave-owners will learn by this that though they may wish to get rid of them, and that though the action of the Whig party has been such as to encourage negro emigration to Ohio, that the people will not tamely submit to be flooded and overrun by their slaves."[5]

Mercer County was primarily settled by German farmers, along with a mix of English, Irish and Scottish immigrants. In 1845, Judge William Leigh of Virginia authorized the purchase of some land on which to place the slaves who had been freed in the will of John Randolph of Roanoke. As Randolph's executor, Leigh hired Samuel Jay of Miami County to buy land. Jay set about purchasing 3,200 acres in the southern part of Mercer County, where there already was a large black settlement, as well as some property near Celina.

John Randolph of Virginia is often touted as a "kindly" slave owner. *Google Art Project.*

When the white residents of this sparsely populated region of the state learned of the plan, they called a meeting and passed a resolution requiring "blacks and mulattoes to give bond, with security, for their good behavior and maintenance, before settling in this State."[6] But that didn't satisfy everyone. In a subsequent meeting, they passed additional resolutions opposing the settlement of blacks anywhere in Mercer County.

On Sunday, July 5, 1846, the refugees, nearly four hundred in number, arrived at New Bremen before daybreak on canalboats, having traveled from Cincinnati. They were accompanied by Thomas Caldwell (or Cardwell), who had been contracted to deliver them to their new home. By noon, word of the ex-slaves' arrival had spread throughout Mercer County, and a large contingent of white citizens had assembled at New Bremen. They were led by Silas Young, Samuel Grunden and Judge Benjamin Linzee. Although New Bremen was a German community, Linzee and Young were not German and none of these men was from the immediate vicinity.

They told Caldwell he would have to remove the former slaves by ten o'clock the next morning. Caldwell asked that they be permitted to remain at their encampment outside town for three days to allow time for Leigh to arrive and take charge of them. He also offered to hand over $1,000 in cash as a surety bond for their good behavior and his promise to depart in three days. However, the offer was refused because the residents feared Caldwell would simply flee and leave the migrants with them.

The exodus of former Randolph slaves may have resembled this illustration. *Authors' collection.*

Caldwell then volunteered to be locked up in the county jail for three days, but they refused that as well. The citizens wanted the ex-slaves taken away by the deadline they had set unless he posted $500 for each of them. Then on Sunday evening, a mob armed with muskets and bayonets marched on the campsite. Taking Caldwell into custody, they left after posting guards around the perimeter of the camp.

Judge Leigh had purportedly agreed to meet Caldwell at New Bremen, but, if unable to do so, he stipulated Samuel Jay was to take charge. But on Monday morning, Jay claimed he did not have written authorization from the judge to do anything. Caldwell was then ordered to make arrangements to transport the former slaves elsewhere. Chartering two boats, he placed his human cargo aboard and departed at noon. They were followed by armed citizens as far as the Mercer County line, so they retreated about twenty-two or twenty-three miles.

The *St. Mary's Sentinel* editorialized,

> *Every reflecting man must see that the establishment of an extensive colony of black in our county must be destructive of the dearest interests and withering to the brightest hops of an honest and industrious people, who have*

Goodrich Giles and Fountain Randolph founded the Randolph Slave Society. *Piqua Public Library.*

endured the privations and hardships of opening farms and establishments for themselves homes in an unbroken wilderness. Such men will not quietly submit to have their farms and hard earnings of the best portion of their lives to be rendered worthless by the settling down amongst them of a colony of manumitted slaves, thus blighting their interests as thoroughly as the settling of a cloud of locusts upon the fair fields of Egypt.[7]

On August 15, 1846, a second meeting was held at New Bremen. This one was for the stated purpose of removing the entire black population from Mercer County (which then included Auglaize County) and ensuring other people of color did not settle there. Francis Miller (some sources say Travis Mueller) was chosen to chair the meeting, and John T. Ferguson was appointed secretary. Both men were residents of St. Marys, about eight miles distant.

The committee unanimously resolved that 1) "the Negroes and Mulattos" came to Mercer County in violation of the law and contrary to the wishes of the white people; 2) the white people did not want to live among people of color and would resist their settlement to the full extent of their means, not excepting the bayonet; 3) the blacks were put on notice to leave by March 1, 1847, or they would be removed by force if necessary; 4) those in attendance would not longer conduct business with the blacks after January 1, 1847; and 5) they pledged to vote for anyone who agreed to support legislation prohibiting the migration of blacks or mulatoes into Ohio.

Meanwhile, the fate of the refugees hung in the balance.

BELMONT COUNTY

Captina or Guinea

CAPTINA, GUINEA OR FLATROCK (SOMERSET TOWNSHIP)

Drewry Betts of Sussex County, Virginia, was a slave owner who had some compunctions about owning slaves. When he penned his last will and testament in 1816, he declared that John W. Watkins, as his executor, was authorized to sell his land, but not his slaves. "It is my will and desire believing freedom to be the natural right of all mankind that after the death of my wife all my slaves namely Peter, Will, Nicholas, Judah, Tempy, Silky and such others as may be found on my estate be emancipated and all their increase as they arrive to the age of 21 yrs."[8]

Presumably, Betts was dependent on slaves to operate his plantation. So despite his belief that freedom was everyone's natural right, he wasn't about to undermine his own livelihood by freeing his slaves while they were still needed to work. However, he directed that once his estate was sold to pay off any debts, the balance was to be divided up among his slaves, with the six previously mentioned receiving three-fifths and the rest of his slaves two-fifths.

The story of one—Silky—was preserved by William G. Wolfe. Before Betts bought her, she was known as Silky White. "Possessing many attractive qualities not common to the average slave girl," Wolfe wrote, "she served in the home as a maid to Mrs. Betts."[9] One of the primary qualities evidenced by most house slaves was a light complexion. They were also the ones most likely to be granted their freedom.

On January 4, 1821, following the death of Mrs. Betts, Silky was issued her emancipation certificate by the Sussex County Court: "The said Silky is of a yellow complexion, five feet and six and a half inches high, has no visible scar on the hands or face, and appears to be about twenty-one years of age."[10] Although Silky was one of eighteen slaves who were to share in the estate, there is little doubt that they were cheated out of much of it. Silky received about one hundred dollars.

"Pinning the money, the precious certificate of emancipation, and a certified copy of her old master's will in the bosom of her dress, [Silky] started towards Ohio."[11] Somehow, she made her way to Captina Creek in Belmont County, where she found others like herself. Silky decided to stay and make it her home. She soon found work with a white family for fifty cents a week. It was Silky's ambition to have a house of her own. With fifty dollars left from her inheritance and another thirty dollars she had earned, she bought fifty acres of land and a cow.

George Turner was another former slave who came to Captina Creek. Being mechanically inclined, he had worked as a blacksmith on his master's plantation. Turner must have worked for others as well, for eventually he saved $300 to buy his own freedom. He then started for Ohio. Not long after he met Silky, they were married and settled down on her farm. In addition to raising crops, he continued to ply his trade as a blacksmith. They also had two sons and a daughter—Margaret.

The Turners were respected members of the farming community, which came to be called Guinea or New Guinea by outsiders—although the residents disliked the name. Later, it was known as Captina and, still later, Flatrock. Other African American households included the surnames Betts, Hargrave, Harper, Newsome, Simmons, Watkins and Wooten.

About 1825, "the colored Methodists of the neighborhood" held the first camp meeting that ever took place in Belmont County. It was in "Somerset township on the head waters of Captina creek, close to the present meeting house of the A.M.E. Captina Church."[12] A church was organized and attracted African Americans from nearby Barnesville. In 1864, it was renamed the Bethel African American Episcopal (AME) Church, which continued to operate for nearly another century before falling into disrepair.

Captina became a station on the Underground Railroad, earning a reputation "as a safe stop where the residents were reportedly well-armed."[13] Alexander L. "Sandy" Harper, formerly of Virginia, was a recognized

About 1825, the "colored Methodists" held a camp meeting on Captina Creek. *Authors' collection.*

Over 6,700 black Ohioans served in the Civil War and for lower pay. *Authors' collection.*

The grave of Underground Railroad conductor "Sandy" Harper at Captina. *Author photo.*

leader—"the heart of it all" according to Mark Morton, who is involved in restoring the cemetery Harper founded.[14] Morton and others have pieced together the stories of some of the many people who have been buried there since 1830. Of the 130 known burials in the cemetery, at least 9 were Civil War veterans.

One of the standing stones in the Payne's Crossing Cemetery was placed in honor of James Betts, a farmer and Union army veteran, and his wife, Rebecca. The Betts surname is significant because it ties Captina to Payne's Crossing, a free black community in Hocking County. Genealogist Sandra Barnes found that the children of Jesse and Mary McKee Payne of nearby Smith Township moved to the Payne's Crossing area before 1860.

Another early settler in Captina was Jeremiah Myers. Born in Baltimore, Maryland, the son of Philip Harper, a man of German ancestry, he came to Ohio in 1825 when he was fourteen. He married his neighbor, Mary Ann Harper, seven years later. The Harpers were also among the original settlers at Payne's Crossing and seem to have had their origin at Captina.

William D. and Jane Harper of Belmont County had four sons and three daughters. One daughter, Rebecca, married a Betts, while son John married Elizabeth McKee in 1830. John and Elizabeth had at least five children, all of whom moved to Michigan, including Catherine B., wife of Thomas W. Cross, who had been liberated in Hocking County by his plantation-owning father.[15]

Like most black settlements, Captina had begun to fade out of existence by the early years of the twentieth century.

BROWN COUNTY

Ripley and the Gist Slaves

RIPLEY (UNION TOWNSHIP)

According to historian Charles Galbreath, "As early as 1796, William Dunlop left Fayette County, Kentucky, and settled in Brown County, Ohio (then in the Northwest Territory). He brought a large number of slaves with him, set them free and 'established them on land about Ripley.'"[16]

Arguably, the most important station on the Underground Railroad, Ripley was founded by Colonel James Poage (or Poague). A slave owner from Virginia by way of Kentucky, Poage had come to abhor slavery. In 1804, he took his family and twenty slaves and settled on one thousand acres of "Survey No. 418 in Ohio, along the Ohio River…and here he made his home and laid out a town, which he named Staunton, for Staunton in Virginia."[17] He then gave his twenty slaves their freedom.

In 1816, Staunton was renamed Ripley after an American general in the War of 1812. During the years leading up to the Civil War, it became the home of many prominent abolitionists, including John Rankin and John Parker, as well as a haven for runaway slaves.

Dr. Alexander Campbell, a native of Virginia, was a physician in Cynthiana, Kentucky. After serving in the Kentucky General Assembly, he "removed to Ripley, Ohio, in 1803, taking with him several slaves and giving them their freedom."[18] An unwavering abolitionist, he was the first of twenty-one vice presidents of the Ohio Anti-Slavery Society.

Ripley abolitionist John Rankin's House in 1936, prior to restoration. *Library of Congress.*

The Reverend Samuel Doak of Tennessee, a Princeton graduate, became "one of the early southern opponents of slavery."[19] Originally from Virginia, he inculcated his beliefs in many of the young men he trained for the ministry, including John Rankin, who married Jean Lowery, one of Doak's granddaughters.[20] Doak was held in such high esteem that he was customarily allowed to cast the first vote in any election. However, it wasn't until about 1818 that the "Presbyterian bishop," as he was called, finally freed his own slaves. Eleven of them relocated to Brown County.

As a result, many small black settlements, such as Africa, were established in the hills above Ripley.

GIST SLAVES

If there ever was a rags-to-riches story it was that of Samuel Gist. Orphaned as a boy in England, Samuel spent his formative years at Bristol Hospital, a charity school. In 1739, he sailed to Virginia at the age of sixteen, hoping to improve his situation. He was indentured to John Smith, a tobacco farmer, and, presumably, learned about business from Smith's position as a factor—or middleman—for a company based in Bristol.

When his employer died in 1747, Gist not only stepped into Smith's job but also married his widow, Sarah (or, perhaps, Mary) Massey and gained control of his enormous wealth. In addition to operating plantations in Amherst, Goochland, Hanover and Henrico Counties, Gist engaged in real estate speculation as a partner in the Dismal Swamp Company. He also dealt in slaves.

After the American colonists declared their independence from Great Britain in 1776, Samuel Gist, a British Loyalist to the end, decided to return home to England. For some reason, he left his wife behind, and she died before she could join him. Six years later, the Virginia Assembly transferred Gist's Virginia holdings, including eighty-two slaves, to his stepdaughter, Mary Anderson. Later, he took legal action to recover his property, though he would never go back to America.

Despite being a slave trader, Gist had, it was said, always been kind to his slaves and never permitted them to be flogged. As he approached the end of his life, he decided he would like to free them upon his death. But he seems to have been conflicted over how best to accomplish this and still provide for his two daughters. So on June 22, 1808, Samuel put his wishes in writing. After ensuring that his daughters would continue to live in the luxury to which they were accustomed, Samuel also made "ample provision for the future of those who had so abundantly filled his coffers by their servitude"—in other words, his slaves.[21]

At the time of his death in 1815, Samuel Gist was believed to be ninety-two years old. His will stipulated that within one year, his slaves would be freed and his property in America sold in order to provide for them and their heirs forever. The trustees charged with executing his instructions were to purchase land for them and build homes, schools and churches. They were also to hire teachers and ministers to instruct them "in the Christian religion according to the Protestant Doctrine as taught in England."[22]

Samuel's daughters immediately sought to manumit three hundred of his slaves in Hanover County, Virginia, in 1815. The following February, the General Assembly of the Commonwealth of Virginia passed an act that authorized the last will and testament of Samuel Gist to be carried out by John Wickham, the surviving trustee. The other, Matthew Toler, died in the interim.[23] However, should there be objections made to relocating the slaves to anywhere with the United States, the General Assembly approved that they "be removed to the coast of Africa, and comfortably established at the free settlement of Sierra Leone."[24]

Predictably, Samuel's heirs and creditors tried to erect roadblocks. The biggest problem was that to some extent, their financial security depended on the slaves not getting their freedom. "If emancipated, the ex-slaves could bring no income to the heirs and could also require expenditures; if held to slavery, the slaves might bring greater income to the heirs."[25] And, by Virginia law, the freed slaves could not remain within the state.

By the time the lawyers were done, the estate had to pay out nearly $30,000 to settle various claims, which drastically reduced the funds available for the resettlement of the ex-slaves. In addition, promised funds from Gist's English estate were never delivered. Some slaves, weary of waiting for justice to be served, ran away, but most of them were recaptured.

Having never felt that he was suited to the job, John Wickham declined the trusteeship, passing the job off to his son, William F. Wickham. Assisted by Carter B. Page (his brother-in-law), William acquitted himself in a reasonably professional manner, given that he supported the institution of slavery. However, he did not do more than was required to uphold Gist's property rights. He would ensure that the former slaves were removed from Virginia and released in a free state.

William Waller Hening, a legal scholar and friend of Thomas Jefferson's, prepared 350 certificates of emancipation that were effective on October 30, 1818. Not long afterward, several Virginians were awarded contracts

The first wave of Gist slaves began arriving by foot from Virginia in 1819. *Authors' collection.*

to deliver the former Gist slaves to three locations in Ohio. The choice of Ohio or Indiana was apparently William Wickham's decision, after rejecting Sierra Leone and Guinea.

Unfortunately, one sentence in Samuel Gist's will would haunt the former slaves and their descendants to this day: "This land must never be sold but must be handed down from one generation to the other."[26]

UPPER CAMP (EAGLE TOWNSHIP)

The Gist Settlement in Eagle Township, Brown County, a few miles north of Georgetown, was the first to be established. Known as Upper Camp, the 1,197-acre tract on Brush and White Oak Creeks was divided into thirty-one lots for the benefit of 150 emancipated slaves. The deed to the property was recorded by the county clerk of courts on August 4, 1819. Sixteen miles to the south in Scott Township, Lower Camp, a sister settlement, was founded a year or two later. The cost of the land for both settlements was $4,400, roughly $87,000 two centuries later.

According to historian Beverly Munford, the initial group of settlers consisted of "one hundred and thirteen from Hanover County and one hundred and fifty from Goochland and Amherst Counties."[27] Among the surnames were Cluff, Cumberland, Davis, Ellis, Fox, Garrison, Gist, Hudson, Johnson (or Johnston), Locust (or Locus), Moss (or Mop), Parsons, Williams, Woodson and York. Per an early county history, they "were all legally warned to depart from the township, lest they should become a township charge."[28]

The former Gist slaves came to Ohio in several waves, and their exact number is unknown. When Samuel Gist returned to England in 1782, he left behind 55 slaves. By 1809, however, the number had increased to 274. And at the time of his death, he purportedly owned 350. A figure of 900 to 1,000 has also been bandied about. His will called for them to be provided with homes, schools and churches, but there is no indication any preparations had been made for them. Certainly, if the standard Brown County history is to be believed,

Their "comfortable homes" lay in the wild region about them; the education they received was in the stern school of adversity. As a matter of course, they did not prosper. Some who were able returned to Virginia. Others built rude

huts and began clearing away the forest. What little money they had was
soon spent. Scheming white men planned to get their personal property.[29]

There are three schools of thought regarding the tracts of land that Gist's agents procured for the former slaves. Either they bought them sight unseen, they were woefully naïve when it came to evaluating its suitability for farming or, perhaps, they were corrupt and were diverting money to their own pockets. But whatever the case, Samuel Gist's estate had already been gutted by the court challenges and the promised funds greatly reduced.

Whatever the truth, the manumitted families were plopped down in the middle of an untamed marshland. "These lands were covered with thickets of undergrowth and sloughs of stagnant water, and were almost valueless at that time for any purpose other than pasturage."[30] In the opinion of Paul Tomlinson, who knew some of the settlers, "They had been raised in the tobacco fields and were totally ignorant of any means of wringing a subsistence out of such a soil, in fact educated white people with their means could scarcely have done so, if at all."[31]

At the risk of being re-enslaved, some of the former slaves returned to Virginia, while many moved to other black settlements or sought out kinfolk elsewhere in Ohio. Bristo Essex, for example, who came to "the camps" when he was four years old, lived in Eagle Township for a couple of years, a couple of more in Highland, returned to Eagle for seven or eight years, then went back to Highland.

Those who remained in Brown County, however, fashioned shelters as best they could and set about clearing the land of brush and woodlands. Although they had some money, it was not enough to sustain them until they could support themselves off the fruits of the land. In short, prosperity would remain just beyond their grasp—at least as long as they stayed on the farm.

However, there were opportunities for those who didn't mind working on the wharf in Cincinnati or on steamboats plying the Ohio River. Eventually, the lure of the city and the prospect of better jobs led nearly all of them to leave. "In 1820," Munford asserted, "three Gist families with twenty-five members lived in the Eagle Settlement while four Gist families with forty-eight members were in the Scott 'camp.' In 1830 eight Gist families with forty-eight members lived in Brown County."[32]

Charles Hammond, editor of the *Cincinnati Gazette*, wrote about his visit to the Gist Settlements in 1835. He described it as an experiment "made

The Gist Settlement probably resembled this one at Trent River, North Carolina. *Authors' collection.*

to test the merits of the negro race under the most favorable circumstances for success."[33] However, it had unquestionably failed. "The two negro settlements are dead weight upon Brown County, as to any productive benefit from negro labor, and that spaces of the county might as well, to this day, have remained in the possession of the Indians."[34]

According to Hammond, "Farms given to them 15 years ago instead of being well improved, and timber preserved for farming have been sadly managed....They are so excessively lazy and stupid that the people of Georgetown (near their camps) and neighboring farmers will not employ them."[35] But when Solomon Hudson died the same year, he owned one hundred acres of land, plows, a wagon, blacksmith tools and "a small number of cows, horses, sheep, calves, hogs, and pigs."[36] Although not wealthy by any means, he was a success.

C.A. Powell and his coauthors suggested that in some cases the Gist settlers were their own worst enemies. "They became involved in numerous law suits among themselves, and so from various causes they were reduced almost to pauperism. In later years, their lands have been sold, so that at present but few families remain as relics of this once large settlement."[37]

People of color found employment on the railroads as cooks and porters. *Authors' collection.*

A century ago, Beverly Munford had this to say about the Gist slaves: "From the best information obtainable, it seems that they were treated in no very friendly manner and that, in time, the negroes lost most of the lands provided for them by their former owner."[38] However, they were victims of the dependent relationship that existed between the former slaves and the executors of Samuel Gist's will.

LOWER CAMP (SCOTT TOWNSHIP)

In 1821, the *Niles Weekly Register* reported that fifty-eight former slaves were en route from Virginia to Brown County. They likely were headed to Lower Camp in Scott Township, the second of the Gist Settlements to be established. By all accounts, these formerly enslaved individuals would be saddled with many of the same problems that faced those at Upper Camp, beginning with poor land, inadequate shelter and insufficient provisions. They also had to cope with open hostility from their neighbors.

This influx of people of color had not gone unnoticed by white settlers, especially those who had migrated from the southern states and were slavery sympathizers. For example, an armed posse of eighteen white men marched on one of the Gist Settlements in Brown County on May 30, 1839. Their intent was to arrest a black man for some unspecified crime. However, "after securing their victim, they commenced whipping a negro woman, who had on a previous occasion, struck one of their number, and she making some resistance on the ruffians raised his gun and shot her in the back."[39] The woman was expected to die. "In justification of this most brutal outrage," the *Lebanon Star* reported, "the offenders put in the plea of *self defence!*"[40]

In 1862, the *Cincinnati Gazette* complained that the freed blacks in Brown County were prone to indolence. An Ohio senator remarked:

> *From the commencement, there has been no improvement in their morals or habits—idleness and vice are the prevailing concomitants. The cost of criminal prosecutions has been very large in proportion to the number of inhabitants, and continues to increase. Within the vicinity of this settlement, there is not a family within two miles who are not kept in constant dread of depredations or injury of some sort. Everything valuable that can be removed is stolen.*[41]

However, not all white men were the enemy. In a letter to Professor Wilbur Siebert, Paul Tomlinson recalled how the Quakers at Fall Creek sent a committee to the colony to check on their needs:

> *They found them needing everything, not least of which was teachers. They took up subscriptions and wagon loads of provisions, such as flour, corn-meal, potatoes, bacon and clothing &c were sent to distribute, Teachers were also sent. A bright young man was brought home and educated—at a private school—for the purpose of supplying the place of teacher. It took years of care and solicitude on the parts of Friends to care for this poor colony. All laws were against them. Any scoundrel could take advantage of them and no colored man could testify in Ohio courts against a white man. No schools were open to them. The society of Friends were nearly their only friends.*[42]

The original settlers of Lower Camp had the surnames Armistead, Clough, Gist, Punch, and Smith. However, Philip Schwarz found that by 1840, the number of settlers using the Gist name had decreased dramatically, with

Barbering was one trade that was generally open to black men. *Authors' collection.*

only thirteen in the Highland Settlement and none in the Eagle or Scott. The most enduring family names were Anderson, Baker, Cumberland, Ellis, Hudson and Turner.

Writing in 1908, sociologist Richard R. Wright Jr., an African American, asserted: "Of the 2328 acres given to these unlettered and untrained people earnest inquiry has failed to find more than a hundred acres now in the possession of their descendants. They were unable to cope with their environment and little by little their land got away from them."[43] A person who described as "a reliable correspondent" informed him that "the remnant of these people live in small huts and labor by the day for their living."[44]

CHAMPAIGN COUNTY

McNeal and Vanmeter Colonies

McNEAL COLONY (SALEM TOWNSHIP)

As early as 1810, Griffith Evans, his wife, Martha, and his family had moved to the vicinity of Mount Tabor, Salem Township. Originally from Greenbrier County, [West] Virginia, they used their "humble cabin, with its dirt floor and puncheon seats" as the first Methodist church in the community.[45] They purchased a large tract of land from a Virginian, Alexander Dunlap, and were soon joined by others from Greenbrier County.

"Mrs. Evans [née McNeal] was a woman of wealth and inherited a number of slaves, but after her marriage she set them all free,"[46] one local historian wrote. It is believed that all of them followed her to Ohio and many settled in the vicinity of the Evans homestead, where their former mistress "used them as kindly as if they had been her own children."[47]

By 1850, a number of African Americans were residing in Salem Township, but it is not known if any of them had a connection to Martha Evans. The most likely prospects were the Gales, Gaters, Gates and Linns, all of whom were born in Virginia (likely West Virginia). Other African American surnames were Artes, Manley and Tabin.

VANMETER COLONY (UNIDENTIFIED TOWNSHIP)

Not all citizens of Champaign County were amenable to having African Americans live among them. When Mad River Township was formed, a resolution was passed declaring that "persons of color should not be allowed to settle in the township."[48] While there is no evidence that it was ever enforced, the attitudes of the residents may have been enough to deter black people from attempting to do so.

On November 5, 1820, three years before he passed away, Abraham Vanmeter of Hardy County, [West] Virginia, wrote his last will and testament. He left one-third of his estate to his wife, Elizabeth, including five slaves: Jacob, George, Solomon, Amelia and Mary. However, he then added:

> *Considering the great hardships of Slavery to which an unfortunate class of beings among us is Doomed, and wishing as much as (in consideration of their faithful Servitude to me) in my power lies to ameliorate their condition: It is my Will and Desire that all my negro Slaves be at my Decease completely Emancipated agreeable to the existing Law of this Commonwealth.*[49]

Abraham also stipulated that "it is my further will and desire that the One Third part of the money arising from the Sale of my personal Estate be equally divided as aforesaid among my Negroes."[50]

In the inventory of Abraham's estate, a family of slaves with the surname Bruce was listed and appraised: Joe, his wife and their ten children were valued at $2,100. According to one genealogist, Joe and Sarah Bruce were the fourth great-grandparents of Dr. Henry Louis "Skip" Gates Jr. on his father's mother's side. Dr. Gates is a renowned historian, literary critic and the host of the PBS television series *Finding Your Roots*.[51]

Upon his death in 1823, Abraham freed seven members of the Bruce family, but five of Joe and Sarah Bruce's children remained "enslaved to his wife Elizabeth Vanmeter until the time of her death."[52] According to Dr. Gates, the Bruces—who were freed upon the death of Abraham Vanmeter—had to file a petition to remain in the state every year. When Elizabeth subsequently passed away around 1840–41, she bequeathed her entire estate to the Bruce family—including one thousand acres and a sawmill.[53]

Records found in the Champaign County Recorder's Office indicate sixteen slaves were emancipated by Abraham and Elizabeth Vanmeter on November 15, 1850.[54] However, no black or "colored" Bruces or Vanmeters appear in the federal census for Ohio. But Solomon Bruce, one of the manumitted slaves, moved to Greene County, Pennsylvania, and is believed to have married Eleanor "Nellie" Lett.

DARKE COUNTY

Long Town

GREENVILLE NEGRO SETTLEMENT OR LONG TOWN (GERMAN/LIBERTY TOWNSHIP)

The original settlers of German (later Liberty) Township, Darke County, were a blend of "Negro, Indian, Danish, Irish, German, English and Dutch," according to historian Steven Miller.[55] A number of them were triracial, a term which refers to people with a mix of African, American Indian and European heritage. Even today, many of their descendants in Darke County refer to themselves as "colored," although many could easily pass for white.

Exactly when the first African Americans began to make their way to Darke County is lost to history. However, the establishment of the Greenville Negro Settlement can be pinpointed with a fair amount of certainty. The story began in 1818 when James Clemens bought some 320 acres or more in Darke County. By 1857, he had expanded his holdings to 920 acres.

Originally from Rockingham County, Virginia, Clemens and his wife, Sophia (or Sophoria) Sellers, were former slaves. They would go on to have ten children: five sons—three of whom became ministers—and five daughters. Not only was Clemens the founder of the black settlement, but he also was "instrumental in starting the first school, donated land for the Wesleyan Church and established a cemetery for the community."[56] Fittingly, his home is one of the few that survives.

James and Sophia Clemens built this Darke County home in 1850. *Author photo.*

Clemens was a prosperous farmer and land owner whose barn still stands. *Author photo.*

Six years later in 1822, Thornton Alexander, also from Rockingham County, bought land in Randolph County, Indiana, about a mile west of the Clemens homestead. Alexander's former master was Adam Sellers—who was in all likelihood Sophia's father. Adam was said to have freed his sixteen slaves about 1816, then moved to Ohio, joining a son who had already settled there.

According to Michael Sellers, a descendant, Adam bought 206 acres for himself from George Harnsberger in Warren County. He then purchased land for his former slaves in Darke County. During a visit to the area in 1909, W.E.B. DuBois, the African American historian and civil rights activist, picked up a bit of oral history concerning a "Pennsylvania Dutchman who went to Virginia and had a daughter too darkly beautiful to marry under Virginia law," while his neighbor "had a son who was born of an Indian Negro squaw."[57]

In 1804, the son walked all the way to Ohio and "squatted" on a piece of land in Darke County. Later, he returned home to marry the Dutchman's daughter before returning to Ohio. Not long afterward, the Dutchman abandoned his white family and followed his daughter to her new home, accompanied by his "colored children."[58] He subsequently lived out his life with his "darker daughter" on the 728 acres they had acquired.

The Dutchman, obviously, was Adam Sellers, whose original surname was likely to have been Zellers. The daughter was Sophia Sellers, and the son was James Clemens. In 1823, they were joined by Reuben Bass and his wife, who came from Guilford County, North Carolina, and settled on 200 acres where they raised eight children. DuBois related, "One white planter brought his colored son and ten grandchildren and placed them on 700, acres, and even as late as 1850, came a white Mississippi planter and two black wives, with fifteen sons and daughter and $3,000 in gold."[59]

Others would quickly follow. Their surnames included Alexander, Bass, Burden, Carpenter, Clemens, Cook, Good, Green, Lewis, Mason, McKenney, Morton, Moss, Okey (or Ochey), Ross, Sanders, Shaffer, Smith, Stokes, Wade and Williams.

In 1845, the Union Literary Institute, a manual trades boarding school, was founded by the antislavery Quakers, as well as Clemens and Alexander. Located on the Indiana side of the border, it opened for business the following summer. The school continued to operate until 1914.

Not surprisingly, there was Underground Railroad activity in Darke County as there tended to be anywhere African Americans came together. It wasn't so much an established railway line as a collection of individuals—the

Clemenses and the Alexanders among them—who were willing to assist any runaways by leading them from one point to another and concealing them when necessary. Some even attended the trade school.

About 1850, a temperance society was formed in the settlement and thrived for a time. Its activities were discontinued not long after the nation was plunged into Civil War in April 1861. Although abolitionist Frederick Douglass had advocated for the use of African American troops in the Union army from the start, it wasn't until May 1863 that the War Department established a procedure for doing so.

Some men from the Greenville Settlement were among the first to enlist, joining the Fifty-Fourth Massachusetts, the first "colored" regiment of the United States Colored Troops (USCT). Roane Smothers identified forty-two graves of black Civil War veterans in the Clemens and Bass cemeteries.[60] Clemens's grandson James R. Clemens, for one, served as a private in the Eighth USCT, an infantry unit. Other surnames were McCowan, Rickman, Coston, Holland, Goins, Wade, Lamb, Patterson, Carman, Candy, Mason, Scott, Cook, Lett, Reed, Shaffer, Archey, Stokes, Davis, Epps and Wesley.[61]

The continual influx of African American migrants and refugees into the Greenville Settlement caused some consternation, as not all proved to be model citizens or felt the same level of investment in the community. "The Wesleyan church," DuBois observed, "split in an attempt to exclude tobacco users and members of secret societies, and wild young lawbreakers and illegitimate children appeared."[62] Furthermore, because many of the residents were exceptionally light-skinned, some fifteen settlement men married white women and moved away, distancing themselves from their black roots.

At its peak, the Greenville Settlement had some nine hundred residents. And as it grew, so did the opposition to its presence. "The surrounding communities," DuBois wrote, "looked with disdain and hatred on these folks whose faces were scarce darker than their own. If a black man came to town he was liable to be chased by hoodlums, and when the whites came out to stop the dedication of a Wesleyan church there was so bloody a battle with fists and brickbats that the experiment was never tried again."[63]

Writing in 1882, historian E. Tucker observed, "The Settlement here lies on both sides of the Ohio line, with by far the largest part in Ohio. In Indiana, a territory about one mile by three is occupied, while in Ohio nearly three miles square is covered by the colored residents."[64] Over the years, "great numbers have emigrated from this 'hive' and gone to other regions to help form new Settlements, or to the towns for reader access

W.E.B. DuBois visited Darke County, possibly in search of his own roots. *Library of Congress.*

to the facilities for work."[65] By the same token, many African Americans with the surnames Lett and Goens (Goins) came to Greenville from similar communities and intermarried.

Tampico was the community's post office from 1850 to 1876 and the closest thing to a town. The only ongoing business conducted there was the selling of liquor. A decade or so later, the local residents began to clamor for a new post office, one that would be more centrally located. They chose the intersection of Hollandsburg-Tampico and Stingley Roads and at first thought they would call the post office "Bethel" in recognition of the Bethel Wesleyan Church. However, when there was opposition to the name, someone suggested "Long" in honor of James and Sarah Long, and it was adopted.

The Longs, a white couple, came to German Township in 1884 and were surprised to find themselves in the middle of a sprawling black community. James had purchased a blacksmith shop sight unseen. Nevertheless, the Longs chose to remain and became highly respected members of Long, or Longtown, as it was sometimes called.

In a letter to the editor of the *Richwood Gazette*, Herbert H. Chavous described a visit to Long in May 1895 while attending an AME District Conference: "On arriving there we found a colored Settlement of rich and prosperous people." They controlled German township, had their own township officer and operated four public schools.

DuBois's description of the Settlement at the time of his visit in 1909 probably differed little from how it was fifty years before. "The land is dark and level," he wrote. "Great fields of corn stand strong and luxuriant. The tobacco is green and silent, and all about are piled sheaves of yellow wheat and oats. Far out in the distance, there are no hills, but only the shadows of oak and beech woods and the dim dying away of level lands."[66] It was an agrarian community from its birth and would remain so, perhaps to its detriment.

DuBois painted a vivid picture:

> *The houses stand from a hundred to a thousand feet apart. Some are old and built with some shade of the style of Southern mansions. Most of them are newer, representing a renaissance of building in the last decade or two....Here is a cottage, with smooth-shaven lawn and flowers; yonder a little, irregular house, with no step, but wandering path and gardens; further on are great barns and a straight, busy house, naked of porch or ornament. There where I stay is a yellow house, surrounded by a porch with climbing clematis, barns and outhouses, and in front a view of great stretches of green corn and tobacco.*[67]

However, one of the most striking aspects of Long was the appearance of its citizens. "Looking at the people first," DuBois observed, "you would have noted little unusual—they were well fed, well dressed, quiet and white. That is, mostly white—here and there a tinge of gold and olive with brown, and one or two black faces."[68] In fact, he estimated fully half of them could blend in with their white neighbors and never be suspected of having "black blood." Long had become something of a sanctuary for interracial couples.[69]

The community began to fade away following World War II. The residents had come to realize they needed to buy equipment to modernize their farms but found that few banks were willing to provide loans.

DELAWARE COUNTY

Depp Settlement and Little Africa

DEPP SETTLEMENT (CONCORD TOWNSHIP)

In 1791, Abraham "Abram" Depp was born a slave in Powhatan County, close by Richmond, Virginia. When he was ten years old, his master, John Depp, a wealthy tobacco farmer, issued a deed of emancipation for him; his mother, Lucinda; and his siblings. John's intent was to grant them five hundred acres in Powhatan County upon the deaths of himself and his wife. However, in May 1806, the law in Virginia changed to require freed slaves to leave the state immediately at the risk of being arrested and sold back into bondage. As a result, the number of manumissions plummeted.[70]

When John Depp passed away in 1831, forty-year-old Abram, a blacksmith by trade, inherited "a handsome little Estate, consisting of both Land and negroes and other personal property."[71] But some of his family members were still held in bondage pending the death of John's wife. Abram petitioned the Virginia General Assembly for permission to remain in Virginia for another two years in order to dispose of his holdings and arrange to leave the commonwealth. His request was granted on March 19, 1832.[72]

Two years later, Abram and his wife, Mary Goode, registered their marriage just prior to his departure for Ohio. Upon his arrival in Columbus, Abram met other free blacks from Virginia. He also became acquainted with abolitionist Joseph Sullivant while working as a blacksmith, only the second one in the state capital. Less than a year later in February 1835,

Fugitive slaves were sometimes hidden in the basement of Abraham Depp's house. *Author photo.*

Elizabeth Depp—John's widow—passed away. During the next two weeks, the remainder of Abram's family sold their land in Virginia and came to Ohio. "At that time there were no railroads from the slave State Virginia to Ohio, a free State. But the determined freemen and their families undeterred by this drawback went forth in covered wagon trains."[73] Those Depps who remained in bondage, however, were sold.

In June 1835, Abram bought three to four hundred acres in Concord Township from Joseph Sullivant. The price was $1,100. Returning to Virginia for his family, Abram started back to Ohio. Before he reached his destination, however, his wife, Mary, died unexpectedly. She was survived by three children, including a son, Aurelius, who attended Oberlin College. Both he and his stepbrother John served in the Twenty-Seventh Ohio Colored Troops during the Civil War.

Three years after his first wife's death, Abram married Chaney Ellis. They would have six children, including Lucinda Depp. When Abram passed away in 1858, his estate was valued at $30,000, making him the richest African American in the county. Although he was the founder of the Depp Settlement, he was not the first African American to settle in the area. John Day was. "He was brought to Ohio a slave, by George Hill, when he came here in 1811, but immediately upon arrival he was given his freedom by Mr. Hill."[74] Eventually, he relocated to the nearby town of Delaware and opened a barbershop.

Other African Americans from the same area of Virginia settled in Central Ohio, not far from Columbus. Among them were James Poindexter (and father Joseph), Archer Goode and Samuel Willis Whyte, along with his son, Dr. Samuel Whyte. "His father bought him and his mother from their master, and then brought them to" the Depp Settlement.[75] Being a mechanic, the elder Whyte purchase just two hundred acres. His son, who became "noted as a specialist of chronic disease," married Louisa Goode, daughter of Archer Goode, known by many as "Saint Louisa" because of her sweet disposition.[76]

James Preston Poindexter came to Ohio with his father, Joseph, at the age of twelve. A former playmate of Dr. Whyte's and a barber by trade, James later relocated to Columbus, where he became a Baptist minister, a civil rights activist and an agent in the Underground Railroad. James also was the first person of color to serve on Columbus's city council and the school board.[77] Other surnames found in the Depp Settlement were Wallace and Meritt.

"The first church building in Concord Township was an old granary, donated for that purpose by James Kooken. Soon after this, A. Depp (colored) put up a log-cabin church on his farm, as a place of worship for the colored Baptists."[78] It became known as Depp's Church. Abram also was involved in the Underground Railroad, hiding fugitives in a limestone cave along the nearby Scioto River. Legend has it that the bell on display at Lucy Depp Park was once used as an "all clear" signal for fugitive slaves.

In 1899, "Robert Goode of Columbus, Ohio, was employed by that city, working at such distasteful tasks as hauling garbage, leveling city dumps, and cleaning streets."[79] He lived in a two-room cottage with his widowed mother. A former slave, she "took in washing to support the family, and with so meager a source of income had great difficulty in keeping her son in school."[80]

At the age of fifteen, Robert was visited by a cousin named Lucinda "Lucy" Depp Whyte who offered to give him a job at her grocery store in Chicago.[81] He jumped at the opportunity and so did his mother. While he worked as a clerk in Lucy's store, his mother found a job with a caterer. "Mother Goode," as she came to be known, returned to Columbus a few years later and opened a successful restaurant.

JAMES POINDEXTER.

Left: James Poindexter became pastor of Second Baptist Church in Columbus. *Authors' collection.*

Below: After Lucy Depp Park became a resort, this barn was used for community events. *Author photo.*

Robert returned as well, working in his mother's establishment for the next eight years. Then in 1922, he had a brainstorm. Lucy Depp "owned a ninety-acre farm, located on the Scioto River about a mile south of the beautiful O'Shaughnessy Reservoir, which had just been completed at that time. One part of this farm faced the river; the other bordered on twin lakes."[82] The land was part of the original Abraham Depp Settlement. The limited farming that took place on it did not generate enough income to pay the taxes. "Hoping that some way might be found to utilize the land in a manner that might benefit her race, she turned to Robert Goode for advice."[83]

After looking the land over, Robert realized that Lucy's acreage would be a perfect vacation spot—Lucy Depp Park. He suggested to her that they develop it as a summer resort for African Americans who lived in the surrounding communities. During the next few years, they had subdivided it into lots, and construction began on houses as well as summer cottages. According to Harry Bailey, who grew up there, Robert "gave the streets the first names of socially prominent black woman of the time—Myrna, Ladona, Gwendolyn."[84] Although she did not live to see it completed, Lucy Depp was pleased to know "that her property would be maintained as a permanent memorial to her"—nearly 185 years after Abraham Depp originally settled here.[85]

LITTLE AFRICA (ORANGE TOWNSHIP)

Samuel Patterson was born in Acworth, New Hampshire, in 1803, and came to Worthington, Ohio, with his parents when he was ten years old. In 1824–25, Patterson, his parents and two sisters, moved to southern Delaware County, where he would live for the remaining years of his life. After purchasing 140 acres of virgin forest land just south of East Orange, Orange Township, Patterson built a double log cabin. The community consisted of eight homes, a blacksmith shop, a general store and a cobbler's shop selling boots and shoes.

The Pattersons lived on the east side of Alum Creek, while "David Patterson, Cyrus Chambers, Thomas McCloud and Nelson Skeels had established their homes on the west side."[86] Not long after he married Hannah Nettleton in 1827, Patterson became a Christian. His grandson Dr. W.M. Hunt wrote, "He exemplified religion in all the walks of life. His integrity was above suspicion. No one ever thought of him as false."[87] In

David Patterson's home was a prominent station on the Underground Railroad. *Author photo.*

1841, Patterson provided his family with a handsome brick house, which still stands, and expanded his farm by another 167 acres.

"In those days," Hunt recalled, "across the creek from East Orange and three hundred yards north, there was a Methodist Church; it stood on a knoll on the west side of the road, with a graveyard back of it."[88] All the members of the East Orange Methodist Church were antislavery in their convictions except for two families. When an abolitionist speaker addressed the congregation in 1847 or so, someone reported the incident to the bishop, who wrote a letter of admonishment and ordered the church members not to do it again. After they did, the bishop came to the church to deliver the "riot act," which ultimately led to the dissolution of that church and the founding of a Wesleyan Methodist congregation. The Wesley Methodist denomination had been organized a half-dozen years before because of conflict over the issue of slavery.

Not long afterward, the proslavery faction "began calling the members of the new church 'Nigger lovers,' and called the village 'Africa' in derision."[89] By and large, the residents of East Orange did not object. Africa, particularly the Patterson home, became a frequented station on the Underground Railroad between Westerville and Mount Vernon.

In 1859, just before the Civil War began, twenty-eight former slaves came to Ohio from North Carolina and settled down in southern Delaware County in the vicinity of Africa or Little Africa, as it was sometimes called. The history of the Alston (or Austin) slaves is related in a paper by Sharon L. Lytle. Her research revealed that the story begins with the birth of Oroondates Davis Alston, son of William and Sarah Yeargan Alston, in 1780. The Alstons were one of the largest slave-owning families in Orange County, North Carolina. "At the age of 9," Lytle noted, "Oroon inherited the family plantation on Seller's Creek, in accordance to his father's will."[90] Census records suggest that he began with about eight slaves, but by the time he passed away in 1851, he owned at least eighty.

In his will, Oroon Alston bequeathed all of his property, real and personal, including his slaves, to his wife, Miriam. However, upon her death, the slaves were to be divided between his four nephews, the sons of his two sisters. Apparently, Oroon and Miriam had no children of their own. Although the Alstons were Methodists, Miriam evidently did not share her husband's views on all things—at least not when it came to slavery.

When Miriam P. Alston made out her last will and testament on September 22, 1855, she disregarded her late husband's wishes and granted all her slaves their freedom. Miriam must have sensed that the end was near, for she died the very next day. Although Miriam was illiterate, she was wise. She willed her slaves to Jesse Marley, her executor, trusting that he would choose the best time to liberate them. In the document, Miriam asserts:

> *It is my will that all the rest of my Slaves shall be free, and I therefore give all my slaves (Abner excepted) to my Executor hereinafter named, in trust that he will remove them as soon after my death as he can lawfully do so to some free state to be there emancipated.*[91]

Miriam directed that Jesse Marley find the freedmen gainful employment until he could take them to a free state. Any money they earned was to be added to the $300 appropriated from her estate to pay for any expenses they might incur on their journey, as well as to compensate Marley and a companion for their time. Since Marley was now their master under the law, they were under his protection and could not be stolen away by slave hunters without violating the Fugitive Slave Act. Not surprisingly, Marley was sued by relatives trying to break the terms of the will. This played out in court during 1857 and into 1858.

Abner, who was more than sixty-eight years old at the time, was left in the care of James Woody for the remainder of his life. Lytle believes that Woody was Miriam's brother-in-law. A power of attorney filed in Randolph County, North Carolina, on April 23, 1859, indicates that by the time Marley decided to take the slaves to a free state, he was no longer healthy enough to do so himself:

> And whereas the said Jesse Marley the duly appointed Executor in said Will, and who qualified, and has acted as such, being in a feeble state of health, and not in a situation to go in person, and convey said slaves to a non-slave holding state, but having settled all said Estate according to law, and being desirous to execute the trust, confided to him in said Will by his said Testatrix, has employed his son Henry B. Marley of Randolph County, to take all said slaves into possession and custody and convey them safely to the State of Ohio, where they may enjoy all the rights of free persons of color.[92]

It would be four years—May 1859—until Marley felt the time was right. With $300 in cash, as well as "teams and wagons," the Alston slaves began their trek to Ohio. Although Oroon had eighty slaves when he died, only twenty-eight are listed on Marley's power-of-attorney, seven of whom were born after Alston was deceased. They had the surnames Alston, Austin, Gains, Dickson, Harris and McField. The disposition of the other fifty-eight slaves is unknown. The power-of-attorney also instructed Henry Marley to transport them to "any part of Ohio which he may deem proper for their benefit and to give them their "Deeds of Emancipation."[93]

Not long afterward, Henry Marley set off to Ohio with at least twenty-eight, and perhaps as many as thirty-five, men, women and children. Jesse had instructed him to hire a helper and take two horse-drawn wagons and a Rockaway carriage for the trip. "They reached and crossed the Ohio River near Portsmouth," Hunt wrote, and arrived in the city on May 15, 1859.[94] The band had managed to traverse half the state of North Carolina, cross the mountains of [West] Virginia and sail down the Ohio River, a distance of more than 360 miles, in about two weeks. They then "came north over the Scioto Trail, and reached the Patterson station during harvest time."[95]

Six days later, Henry completed the emancipation papers. Upon their arrival in East Orange, the freedmen and women were delivered to the home of Samuel Patterson. Because the local farmers needed help bringing in their crops, they persuaded the refugees "to remain there, each family moving into one of several vacant log cabins, and there they stayed for several years, attending the church along with the whites."[96] According to Lytle, "The freed Alston slaves became landowners, musicians and artists and also participated in hiding runaway slaves who travelled to the village. Their descendants served in the military and became educators."

Hunt wrote that the African Americans begin to disperse about 1867, just after the conclusion of the Civil War. One family settled in Delaware, while others headed to Van Wert and Paulding Counties. More than a century later, the creek was dammed to form Alum Creek Reservoir, whose waters cover much of the original crossroads village. Several cemeteries had to be relocated, including Africa Cemetery, where Samuel Patterson was buried.

GALLIA COUNTY

Poke Patch and Lambert Lands

POKE PATCH OR STEWART SETTLEMENT (GREENFIELD TOWNSHIP)

In Greenfield Township, on the Lawrence County border, Irish immigrants Daniel Faulkner and Nancy Dunlop, his wife, built the first cabin in 1806. The first religious services were conducted in a log building on their farm. James Averill recorded in his history of Gallia County that "a colored Baptist, Rev. James Stuart, was the first minister, and he is remembered with feelings of respect, as a thorough Christian, who labored earnestly for the good of the early settlers."[97] This was likely James B. Stewart.

"The second church building," Averill noted, "was erected of round logs, and located on Dirty Face creek, by a party of colored people who came from Tennessee."[98] These would have been the residents of a black community known as Stewart Settlement or Poke Patch, just south of present-day Oak Hill.

The African Americans who settled there included freedmen and fugitives. They found employment at the local iron furnaces or with area farmers. The Stewarts—James B. and Fannie Dungey—were a freeborn black family originally from Virginia that consisted of five sons: John S. (possibly J.), T.N, James W., Isaac and Jacob. All, but especially John and his wife, Eliza Ann Harris, would become involved in the Underground Railroad. His employer was John Campbell, the founder of Ironton.

Communities such as Poke Patch may have existed solely to aid fugitive slaves. *Authors' collection.*

Poke Patch was a key station on the Underground Railroad with liberty lines running to Burlington, Ironton, and Proctorville. As historian Clement Martzloff observed, "There were many well-defined routes of travel through Ohio, upon which people lived who were always ready to hide slaves for a time and then aid them on their way. Their stopping places were called stations, and the people conductors."[99] However, it was in no way as organized as many people believe. "The 'Underground Railroad' was like the guinea-pig," Martzloff wrote, "neither a pig nor a guinea."[100]

During this period, Poke Patch allegedly provided assistance to as many as two hundred fugitive slaves. "Every resident of Poke Patch it would seem was involved in some manner in this clandestine protest against human bondage."[101] One escaped slave, Henry Hutchinson, who remained in Poke Patch, went on to enlist in the U.S. Colored Troops. However, apart from the community's role in the Underground Railroad, very little is known about it. It was never a large settlement, and the religious among them made use of the nearby Union Baptist Church in Blackfork. When the congregation built a new log church in 1879, they located it in Poke Patch. Forty years later, a new church was built on top of Niner Hill.

There were other Stewarts who settled in Poke Patch. Richard Stewart, from Powhatan County, Virginia, moved to Gallia County by 1830. He likely was related to Reverend James Stewart. Richard's daughter, Frances Ann, was born in "Greenfield" in 1832. Her ancestry has purportedly been traced to "the Sapponi and Pamunkey tribes of Virginia."[102] Several of her brothers were pioneers in settling the black community in Cass County, Michigan.

As Cheryl LaRoche pointed out, communities such as Poke Patch "were not 'towns' per se, but rather a loosely knit system of farmsteads spread over the rural landscape usually within a five-miles radius."[103] Poke Patch ceased to exist in the early 1900s, disappearing into the Wayne National Forest.

LAMBERT LANDS (MORGAN TOWNSHIP)

In Bedford County, Virginia, Charles Lambert Jr. passed away in 1839. His will read, "Upon my death, all my black people shall be set free."[104] It also included a list of the emancipated slaves and their original surnames. For example, Frank Lambert was actually Frank Jones.

Bedford County was a hotbed for itinerant slave traders. "From there, coffles of slaves were 'took to Lynchburg, Va., to the block to be sold.'"[105] The year after Charles Jr. died, seventy-three citizens of Bedford County were said to own at least twenty slaves. By the time the Civil War broke out, slaves represented more than 40 percent of the total population. The line between black and white America was plain to see.

Yet Charles distinguished himself by choosing to free his slaves. In the 1820 federal census, he is shown to be living alone with eleven of them. Ten years earlier, he had eighteen. This suggests that he may have engaged in some slave trading himself. He maintained his slaves to support him on his farm and did not feel a need to bequeath them to anyone else. "His last will and testament also stipulated that the freed slaves be given horses, oxen, wagons, clothing, and financial support to help them relocate to a state chosen upon advise [sic] of the will's executors."[106]

"It took four years for the executors of Charles Lambert Jr.'s will to secure the funds that his emancipated slaves would need to make their journey from Virginia to the land where they could live in freedom," the *Gallia Herald* later reported. "Virtually everything in the Lambert estate was sold, including the dining silver."[107]

As a result, in November 1843, formerly enslaved persons led by Frank Lambert settled in Ohio. Frank likely had held a leadership role on the Lambert plantation, perhaps assisting Charles Jr. with its management. "Three deeds in the files of the Gallia County recorder indicate that 265½ acres originally were purchased in Morgan Township for the ex-slaves.… Listed as the purchasers were Frank Lambert and 29 others, all with the surname Lambert."[108] However, they soon began to differentiate themselves by adopting other surnames: Burks, Jones, Leftwich, Miller, Minnis, Randolph, Reed, Sale and Wingfield.

Morgan Township, site of the Lambert Lands Settlement, as it became known, was organized in 1818. It was not the Garden of Eden. In an article for the *Columbus Dispatch*, reporter Bob Waldron spoke with some of the slaves' descendants. They have "'some good timber on them,' one remarked, 'and a quantity of limestone, but the soil itself is nothing to brag about.' The early families raised gardens and some crops, but most of the area since had grown up in burr and weeds."[109] However, it was their new home, and they set about making the best of it.

One direct descendant, the "Rev. Calvin Minnis, 66, said the Lambert community quickly built a school and a church—Morgan Bethel— where he still pastors today. The original building was lost to fire in 1995, but survives in cement-block form next to the cemetery, which is across the hill from where the Lambert Lands begin."[110] The only remaining headstone of one of the original thirty Lambert settlers is that of his grandfather Calahill Minis, who spelled his last name with one *n*.

Although they jointly owned the land, the individual families began to mark off sections as their personal property. Over the years, some asserted squatter's rights to legal possession of the land. In 1938, "the late Robert G. West obtained clear title to a piece of the land through a friendly court suit in which 26 neighbors gave their consent to West's claim. The defendants included such family names as Miller, Minnis, Ellison, Jones, Ealy, Guthrie, Robinson, Norman, Harris and West."[111]

Like many black settlements, Lambert Lands residents assisted hundreds of fugitive slaves on their way to freedom. Some may have even remained with them for a while. But as the original settlers died off, the later generations did not necessarily feel the same attachment to the community. It was hard to make a living there, and many of them scattered to the winds in search of jobs. This presented a difficulty for those who remained behind.

"Years ago in the communal settlement it was the custom for one of their number to collect the real estate tax from the others and pay the

Above: Lambert Lands Cemetery in Gallia County is all that remains of the settlement. *Author photo*.

Left: The Lambert Lands marker list the names of those buried there. *Author photo*.

bill at the country treasurer's office," Pearl Cordell told the *Columbus Dispatch* in 1963. "Nowadays, with the co-owners so scattered, the system has fallen down. I don't know what to do."[112] As families moved away, "unpaid property taxes mounted up, and the Lambert Lands were sold on the Gallia County courthouse steps in 1969."[113] The saga of Lambert Lands came to an end—almost.

In 2002, the Estivaun Matthews, among others, established the Lambert Land Preservation Society. "It was her wish to identify the names of those buried in the unmarked graves at Morgan Bethel Church Cemetery, which is near Lambert Land."[114]

GREENE COUNTY

Brown's Settlement and Others

BROWN'S SETTLEMENT (CAESARSCREEK TOWNSHIP)

According to Greene County historian Wilhelmina Robinson, Revolutionary War veterans who occupied land in the Virginia Military Tract, which included part of Greene County, were sometimes accompanied by their slaves. But since slavery was prohibited by the Northwest Ordinance and, later, the Ohio constitution, they would then set them free. Robinson wrote that these freed slaves tended to congregate in Wilberforce, Yellow Springs, New Jasper and Xenia, while steering clear of proslavery forces in Cedarville.

Frederick Bonner was both a slave owner and a devout Methodist. At the age of forty-two, Bonner sold his five-hundred-acre estate in Tidewater, Virginia, and purchased two tracts of one thousand acres each in Ohio. Then on April 1, 1803, he set off with his family, some friends and a few African Americans to their new home just a couple of miles south of Xenia. Upon reaching his destination, Bonner freed his slaves—with a "clear conviction of the injustice and criminality of depriving my fellow creatures of their natural right"—and established a Methodist community.[115]

Documents on file in the recorder's office attest that many of the African Americans who settled in Greene County, such as Godfrey Brown, were freed blacks who came there on their own:

Brunswick County, [Virginia]: I do hereby certify that the bearer hereof Godfrey Brown a free man of colour aged fifty-two years about five feet ten and one-half inches, yellow complexion, has two scars on his left arm near the elbow carries the mark of small pox on the face and was emancipated by John T. Bowdin as will appear by reference to the deed of emancipation duly recorded in the county aforesaid. Given under my hand this seventh day of March 1820. R. Turnbull, C.B.C.[116]

While still enslaved, Godfrey—a shoemaker by trade—had hired himself out to other planters and was able to save the incredible sum of $5,650 (nearly $122,000 today), with which he purchased not only his own freedom but also that of his wife, Jane Chaney, and a dozen members of his family. It had taken twenty-three years. Two years after he bought his freedom, Godfrey emancipated his wife and four of his children: Sarah "Sally," Moses, Samuel and Rebana (or Bibanah). The others—Richard "Dick," Godfrey, Myles, Elizabeth, Polly Edwards, Joseph and Julia—would receive their freedom when they attained the age of twenty-one. Before leaving Virginia for Ohio, Godfrey, age fifty-two, bought 254 acres in Caesarscreek Township for $1,000 from Brunswick County residents Edward and Sarah C. Bromgoolc.[117]

Upon their arrival in Caesarscreek Township in the summer of 1822, Godfrey and his sons constructed a home for the family in what would come to be called Brown's Settlement (now known as Maple Corner), six miles south of Xenia. He and his eldest son, Samuel, then chose a patch of ground between two branches of a stream and laid the foundation of a church. When the structure was completed, Godfrey named it the Middle Run Baptist Church, purportedly the first African American Baptist church in Ohio. Despite being illiterate, Godfrey would serve as minister of the church for twenty-four years. It also was a station on the Underground Railroad.

Accompanied by Samuel, Godfrey began traveling throughout the state, preaching the word of God and inviting other free blacks to join them at their community. At its peak, Brown's Settlement purportedly had a population of more than one hundred families. In addition to Brown, other prominent surnames were Baker, Green, Hightower, Jackson, Perry and Pierson.

Godfrey and Samuel visited other black settlements in Ohio, including East Wren in Van Wert County. Both of them purchased several tracts of land that were later occupied by Samuel's sons, William H. Brown and James R. Brown. Over the course of two decades, Godfrey would come to own 254 acres in Caesarscreek Township, as well as 80 acres in Township

Caesar's Creek Pioneer Village contains homes from the same era as Brown's Settlement. *Author photo.*

No. 7, Shelby County (purchased in 1833); 160 acres in Willshire Township, Van Wert County (1837); and 160 acres in Hoaglin Township, Van Wert County (1839).

In 1900, the *Xenia Daily News* printed a couple of anecdotes regarding Godfrey Brown. In one, he rebuked Aaron Harlan, a prominent attorney, for laughing at him while he was preaching in the county courthouse. After thanking everyone else for their good behavior, he pointed at Harlan and said, "Dat man dat set right dar he behave monstrous ugly, monstrous ugly, he laugh in de house o God."[118] It should be noted that newspapers of the era often exaggerated black dialect, Sojourner Truth's "Ain't I a Woman?" speech being the most egregious example.

Godfrey passed away in 1843. Following his death, "A section of land was set apart for 'God's Acre,' where their dead might rest near," family historian Harvey Brown wrote.[119] Godfrey remained strong in his faith until the end, as is evidenced in his will: "I commit my Soul to God and my body to the Earth to be decently buried and all my funeral expenses paid. As to debts, thank God I owe no man anything but love."[120]

Samuel Brown married twice. His first wife was Elizabeth Lucas, his second Elizabeth Brandom, an Irish woman. Not only did he raise nine children of his own, but he "also raised three homeless boys that he inspired and trained as Ministers; Rev. Peter Everett, Rev. Samuel Thomas and Rev. Alexander Woodley."[121] One son, Lincoln F. Brown, patented a bridle bit in 1892 and authored a slim volume titled *Jesus Christ and His Way—The True Way or the Way of Truth*. In addition to the 60 acres he inherited from his father in Greene County, Samuel purchased an additional 241 acres in Van Wert County.

Godfrey Brown Jr., Samuel's brother, married Keziah Smith, by whom he had three children. Because he died five years before his father, his inheritance of 160 acres of land in Wilshire Township, Van Wert County, passed to his children.

According to Ida B. Shields, "For many years the colored people of Xenia and vicinity used to go to Brown Settlement to great basket meetings, where the gospel was preached and many rejoiced in serving the Master."[122] In 1889, the congregation of Middle Run Baptist Church moved to Xenia, where they built a new church. By that time, the settlement had run its course.

TAWAWA SPRING OR WILBERFORCE (XENIA TOWNSHIP)

Tawawa Springs, just outside the town of Xenia, was named form a Shawnee word for "clear or golden water." It was also known as Xenia Springs and, for a time, Drake's Springs. In 1850, the land was purchased by attorney Elias Drake, who marketed it as a health resort modeled after White Sulphur Springs north of Columbus. By July 1851, letters were appearing in various newspapers praising its benefits. The same year, a party of homeopathic practitioners came to Ohio to make a tour of the water cure facilities. Although they praised the "fine buildings," expensive furnishings and handsome grounds at Tawawa House, they lingered but a few hours because they "felt so chilled by the cold, frosty air of aristocracy which pervades the whole concern."[123]

At some point, Tawawa Springs caught the attention of southern planters, who decided it was the perfect place to vacation with their enslaved mistresses. They came from as far away as New Orleans. Some of them brought their mistresses, children and servants; purchased farms for them to settle on; and gave them their names and their freedom. Anderson Lewis, a southern slave owner, built Lewis House for his manumitted slaves.

The *Evening Star*, a Washington, D.C. newspaper, published a racist attack on Tawawa Springs in August 1854. It noted that it attracted "the dusky shades of society," although the "pure air and water" did little to improve "their complexions."[124] The writer concluded, "If the weather continues warm, they will have a very agreeable time, if Sambo and Miss Dinah do not use cologne or any other artificial perfume."[125]

Although Tawawa Springs was a delightful setting for a summer resort, it never recouped its cost. In the autumn of 1856, the General Conference of the Methodist Church adopted a resolution to establish a college for people of color. The body purchased Tawawa Springs, "including fifty-two acres of ground, the large hotel with two hundred rooms and much valuable furniture, and six cottages" for the sum of $13,500.[126] Considering that the resort had cost more than $50,000 to build, it was a bargain.

Originally, the school was going to be called the Ohio African University, since it would serve black males, but instead it was christened Wilberforce University. The existing buildings were adapted into dormitories, classrooms, administrative offices and staff residences. From its opening to its closing in 1862, Wilberforce had a student body composed primarily of the mixed-race children of southern slaveowners. With the outbreak of the Civil War, however, they were no longer sent to school in Ohio. A year later, it was purchased by Daniel A. Payne on behalf of the African Methodist Episcopal Church for $10,000 and reopened.[127]

The importance of Wilberforce University in black history cannot be overstated. As the oldest college in the United States founded by African Americans, its original mission was to provide educational opportunities for people of color at a time when few were available to them.

Noah Spears was one of 960 slave owners in Bourbon County, Kentucky. He was the son of Jacob Spears, a pioneering distiller and horse breeder in Bourbon County. After B.W. Stone, a Methodist minister, stopped by in 1855 and railed against the evils of slavery, Noah decided he could no longer own another human being. The following year, he freed his sixteen slaves and built cabins for them on a small parcel of land he had purchased in the vicinity of Tawawa Springs. Spears's former slaves included Green Smith; Harriet Smith; Harriet's children, James and David; and Sanford Williams.

In addition to giving them several hundred acres of land, Spears "came to visit them, equipped each farm with the latest improved farm implements, gave them horses, and distributed among them on two occasions more than $10,000."[128] However, as the Civil War heated up, he felt he could no longer stay in Kentucky, so he fled to Ohio with his wife and family. His kindness to his former slaves was repaid when they gave him and his family shelter.

Abvoe: Wilberforce College occupied the grounds of the former Tawawa Springs resort. *Library of Congress.*

Left: Hallie Q. Brown was one of many distinguished black faculty at Wilberforce University. *Authors' collection.*

Late in December 1856, Joshua Land of Amite County, Mississippi, came to Greene County, Ohio, and signed the manumission papers for Mary Land, his slave of thirty years, and her seven children. He wanted them "to enjoy all the rights to which free white people are entitled by the laws of the State of Ohio and any or all the State of the Union [*sic*]."[129] At the time, Mary was about thirty-four years old, and she had been his property for all but four years of her life.

The fact that one of Mary's children was named Joshua raises questions about the boy's paternity that cannot be answered with any certainty. However, if Mary, an enslaved woman, was also taken as his mistress, he would neither have been the first nor last to enter into such a relationship. In the manumission document, he affirms that he is releasing her "in consideration of friendship and affection."[130]

Another Bourbon County slaveholder, Washington Webb, freed Patty Hurley, her daughter Polly Ann Smith and Polly's children early in 1860. Census records show the former slaves settled in Xenia Township, taking up residence with a woman named Tennessee, age forty, and a man named J.K. Douglas, age seventy.

Although William F. Smith was born in Kentucky, his story really begins in Clinton, Mississippi, where he made his living as a merchant while attempting to make a killing as a real estate speculator. By 1850, he owned a large cotton plantation and ninety slaves. One of them was a woman named Laura Ann. Five years later, William traveled to Greene County, Ohio, accompanied by Laura, age thirty-two, and her (likely their) seven children. He was experiencing financial difficulties again and wanted to place his family beyond the reach of his creditors.

On July 22, 1858, William filed emancipation papers with the Greene County Recorder's Office. The children, all of whom had light complexions, were William, James Dick, Margina, Robert, Edward, Clark and Joseph Smith.[131]

Hallie Q. Brown, the African American educator, later wrote about Smith's arrival in Greene County:

> *To this famous spot* [an old roadside inn] *came, with his family, Captain Smith, owner of an immense former slave plantation, from Mississippi.... The inn was converted into a residence and the surrounding land purchased as a farm and the Smith family comfortably settled. Soon after, the Captain returned to his plantation, taking with him his eldest sons.*[132]

Laura Smith and her children lived comfortably in Wilberforce until her death in 1871 at the age of forty-seven. Her estate would have been worth about $800,000 in today's dollars.

In 1858, James Cotton of Claiborne County, Mississippi, brought Hannah Cummings Cotton, a thirty-nine-year-old slave, to Greene County, Ohio, along with her seven children. He then set them free in exchange for a payment of one dollar. At the same time, he freed James Cummings Cotton, age sixty-three, and his wife, Tamar Cummings Cotton, age sixty-eight, and settled them on a farm he has purchased near Wilberforce University.

Two years later, the 1860 census shows Hannah, her parents and children, including a two-year-old son, living together with Tillman and Lucy Prattis. John Cummings Cotton was now going by the name John Fallor. James Cotton was part owner of Belmont Plantation in Claiborne County along with his brother Thomas. Together, they owned more than one hundred slaves.

Philip Piper was a well-to-do slave owner from Tensas, Catahoula Parish, Louisiana, who took one of his slaves, Nellie (or Nelly), as his mistress.[133] Surprisingly, since many of the slave women taken as concubines tended to have lighter complexions, Nellie was described as "a colored woman darker than a mulatto." In 1859, Piper brought Nellie and their four children to Ohio, gave them their freedom and purchased land for them in Xenia Township in the vicinity of Wilberforce. He then returned home to Louisiana, where census records show him living with his overseer and sixteen slaves.

A year later, Philip, who was fifty, and Nellie, who was thirty-seven, were married in Pennsylvania, where mixed race marriages were legal. They then returned to Greene County. Many of their children went on to attend Wilberforce University. When he passed away in 1879, Philip left his estate to Nellie and their six children.

In 1860, Joseph J. Todd traveled to Ohio from Shelby County, Tennessee, with the slaves of his recently deceased father, John B. Todd. Once there, he proceeded to release them in Greene County. They included Judy Todd; Helen M. Todd; Helen's son, George Lucas; and three young adult men who presumably were Judy's sons.

As was true of many black settlements, the land purchased for and by the former slaves frequently did not remain in the family's possession. African American sociologist Richard Wright observed:

The tax books before 1875 show several estates of a hundred acres or more, owned by the black families of Southern white men. But these have nearly

Massies Creek Cemetery is the final resting place of many Wilberforce pioneers. *Author photo.*

all lost their land. Their children were as a rule extravagant and conceited. I am informed that none were ever graduated from Wilberforce University, which was in their midst.[134]

However, when Booker T. Washington visited Wilberforce in 1906, he was especially taken by was the "air of permanence and stability about this community"—the feeling that "a certain number of coloured people had found themselves, had made a permanent settlement on the soil and were at home."[135]

CONWAY COLONY (MIAMI TOWNSHIP)

Even as social reformer Robert Owens was establishing a "utopian" community in New Harmony, Indiana, another band of Owenites led by Daniel Roe, minister of the New Jerusalem Church, headed for an area just outside Xenia in Greene County. Roe's group, consisting of about one hundred families, purchased 729 acres of land in 1825, including a well-known medicinal spring with yellow-colored waters. Like the New Harmonists, the Yellow Springs group were thinkers and not doers. As R.S. Dills noted in *History of Greene County, Ohio*, "Too soon did the majority assume to be leaders, and issue commands, while an insignificant minority did the work."[136] The community soon dissolved.

However, the arrival of the Little Miami Railroad in 1846 provided a much-needed economic boost to the village, and in 1856, it was finally incorporated. Owing to the mineral springs and a picturesque glen, Yellow Springs became a favorite retreat for city people. In the early 1800s, Lewis Davis and others purchased the area around the springs and developed it as a resort. Wealthy Cincinnatians arrived by stagecoach to vacation at Davis's inn and enjoy the supposedly curative waters.

When Attorney Elisha Mills of Cincinnati learned that the land around Yellow Springs was for sale, he bought it. He began advertising his "water cure" resort, a day's ride from Cincinnati, in 1829. Elisha's son, William, was especially interested in the economic development of the community and would go on to establish Antioch College in 1852. In the meantime, Mills had sold the resort to a Mr. Neff of Cincinnati, who continued to operate it as the Yellow Spring Water Cure Establishment. However, after the property passed through several more hands, including that of Thomas and Mary Nichols, advocates of "free love," it was destroyed by fire in 1862.

The same year, Moncure Daniel Conway led a large contingent of slaves from Falmouth, Virginia, to Yellow Springs. Their number is most often given as thirty-one, but that represents only those slaves who were the property of Moncure's father, Walker. Altogether, Walker owned between fifty and sixty slaves, but nearly half of them had been hired out. As a result, they were trapped behind Confederate lines and unable to escape. A few slaves belonging to a couple of neighbors also made the journey. In his own writings, Conway pegged the number at between forty and fifty, not counting babies and children.

At an early age, Moncure Conway became a staunch antislavery man. In *Testimonies Concerning Slavery*, he wrote of his reluctance to answer when slaves would ask him how they could gain their freedom. Conway was concerned that if they tried to escape and failed, they would either be killed or sold downriver to the Deep South. So he would tell them he "could give them no advice, but if I should ever meet any of them in Cincinnati, where I resided, I would do my best to place them beyond the reach of danger."[137]

When the Civil War broke out, Conway received a letter from his sister that one of their father's slaves, Dunmore Gwinn, had been spotted in Washington City (in other words, D.C.). Worried about Gwinn's welfare, Conway rushed to the capital and began to search for him. Within a few days, Conway discovered that his father's household servant had taken up residence in Georgetown with Eliza, his wife, and their daughter and baby.

In less than a month, Dunmore Gwinn had opened a "small cake-and-candy store, taken in washing, and managed, quite illogically, to get a comfortable home in their few weeks of freedom."[138] And the other "contrabands" were doing equally as well. In fact, Gwinn told Conway that all of his father's slaves had escaped to freedom except for those who were still behind the military lines established by the Union army.

Believing that the fugitives would be severely punished if recaptured, Conway resolved to go to Falmouth and take them somewhere safer. Before he had the chance to depart, however, a terrible storm blew up. To his surprise, he found that all of this father's slaves were concealed in the cellar of a Georgetown home in which he sought refuge, having arrived ten minutes before he did. As a result, Conway was spared having to make a trip to Stafford County.

Since Conway had no title to the slaves, there was a risk they could be stolen from him. The best he could do was obtain a letter from Secretary of the Treasury Salmon P. Chase granting him military protection while passing through Baltimore toward the railroad depot. There were also rumors abroad that slaveholders were moving their slaves out of Maryland in an attempt to evade the emancipation order, and Conway was concerned that he would be mistaken for one of them and attacked. However, the former slaves in his company quickly cleared up any misunderstanding, and it became a "triumphal process" until they encountered a gang of "ugly whites."[139] After a prolonged and uncomfortable delay, he was able to purchase tickets for the train and they set off for Yellow Springs.

Moncure Conway was a friend and admirer of Horace Mann, Antioch College's first president. He knew that Mann had been an ardent antislavery man and nourished a community of free thinkers in Yellow Springs until his death in 1859. He trusted that the former slaves would be welcome in such a place.

Once they arrived in Yellow Springs, the band of freedmen and women—bearing the surnames Berk, Bray, Dunnaho, Grims, Gwinn, Herod, Holmes, Humstead (or Hempstead), Morgan, Parker, Taylor and Wormsley—were housed in a large barn owned by Moses Grinnell. They then set about building houses along the Little Miami River, north of town. Although they had left the plantation system behind in Falmouth, Dunmore and Eliza Gwinn remained the acknowledged leaders. They were joined by Richard Herod, who was the slave of Dr. Lawrence B. Rose and served as his coach driver.

According to Norman Schools, Richard Herod married Nancy Butler Gwinn, the daughter of Dunmore and Eliza Gwinn. Whether Dr. Rose was aware of it or not, when Conway left Falmouth with the slaves in mid-July 1862, Herod joined his wife and their daughter, Elizabeth. A year later, Herod helped organize the First Baptist Church, also known as the Anti-Slavery Baptist Church, along with sisters Naomi McKee, Isabelle Newman and Evelyn Hill   all descendants of the Conway Colony. It was followed by the Central Chapel African Methodist Episcopal Church in 1866. Then in early 1865, Herod enlisted as a private in Company M, Fifth U.S. Colored Heavy Artillery, and he served for a year.

Among the earliest black families to settle in Yellow Springs were Abner and Betsy Morton, who were already in the area by 1835. Wheeling Gaunt (or Gant) may have been the most successful of the group. Born a slave in Carroll County, Kentucky, in 1815, he purchased his own freedom through hard work and frugality, as well as that of his wife, Amanda, and son, Nick.

Within the next few years, Wheeling bought a nine-acre farm for his home and a number of other rental properties. Several years before he passed away in 1894, he made out a will in which he left the rental properties with eight houses, valued at $40 to $50,000 to Wilberforce University and the farm to the Village of Yellow Springs. When Gaunt passed away at the age of eighty-two, he "was thought to be the richest colored man in Ohio."[140]

After living abroad for many years, Moncure Conway returned to the United States in 1875 and made a stop at Yellow Springs "to visit our family negroes, colonized there during the war."[141] He was greeted warmly by the leaders of the community, Dunmore and Eliza Gwinn, who gave a banquet in his honor. Although Conway was no doubt pleased by his reception, he was troubled by "the size and completeness of the mythology which had in twenty-one years formed in the minds of these humble friends."[142] They portrayed him as this outsized heroic figure by putting words in his mouth he didn't say and attributing actions to him he did not perform.

Unlike many of the former slaves who settled in Wilberforce, those who came to Yellow Springs did so of their own accord. They weren't generally sponsored by a former master. "Instead," Wilhelmina Robinson wrote, "they represented more of the free-willed, independent type who purchased their freedom with their own latent talents or escaped slavery through the aid of the abolitionists. They became an integrated part of the white community and shared in the growth and development of the area."[143]

HIGHLAND COUNTY

Gist Settlement or Dark Town

GIST SETTLEMENT OR DARK TOWN (FAIRFIELD/PENN TOWNSHIP)

Having already established two settlements in adjoining Brown County, William Wickham, the agent for the Gist estate, turned his attention to establishing one more:

> *Expensive though it was to obtain new land,* [William F.] *Wickham agreed to the payment of $88 for a 100-acre tract in in Fairfield Township (now Penn Township), northwestern Highland County, about eighteen miles north of the Eagle Township settlement, and near today's Ohio Route 28 along Gist Settlement Road. In 1831 forty-four people were "sent" the new tract. Wickham further agreed in 1835 to pay for 107 more acres of adjacent land.*[144]

The land bought for them was part of the Virginia Military district—land the State of Virginia received in exchange for giving up its claims to other lands as requested by the federal government. "An act of congress and the Virginia legislature granted the reserved land to Revolutionary soldiers who wanted to settle in the 'west.'"[145] However, many preferred to sell it.

The estate agent subsequently divided the property into thirty-one lots and divvied them up among the twenty-eight different families. The first Dark

Town settlers, as they were pejoratively called, had the surnames Brooks, Buford, Carey, Day, Essex, Good, Hailstock, Lawrence, Lawson, Mitchell, Rollins and Turner. It was the smallest of the three Gist Settlements. Located near Dunkard and Quaker families in Snow Hill and High Top, the former slaves were likely treated better there than if they had been placed close to other white communities.

In 1840, the Highland County settlement consisted of eighteen families totaling 105 persons. "Between 1840 and 1930," Laura Richards found, "an average of 16 families, or 75 persons occupied the Gist Settlement (based on US Census Data, 1840–1930)."[146] Until the mid-1840s, the trustees of the Gist estate paid the property taxes and provided other benefits, but at some point the trust became insolvent. The residents of the settlement either did not have the money to pay the taxes or felt they were not responsible for them since they did not hold deeds to the land.

In 1851, the Ohio General Assembly passed an act declaring that "the court of common pleas of Highland county shall have jurisdiction, in the manner hereinafter specified, over the trust funds created by the last will and testament of Samuel Gist, late of England, deceased."[147] The trustees appointed by the court in Richmond, Virginia, and residing in Ohio were ordered to "regularly present to the court of common pleas of Highland county, their accounts and vouchers, for settlement with said court, in the same manner as executors are required to do by law; and they shall, in the management and disbursement of said trust funds, be subject to the same control and supervision of said court of common pleas, that executors appointed by said courts are."[148]

Testifying before the Highland County Court of Common Pleas in 1855, some of the Gist Settlement residents swore that they "received inadequate supplies and meat unfit to eat and that many old and infirm people had to beg around the county to provide for themselves."[149] A year later, several white witnesses asserted that the black settlers, both young and old, were continually begging for assistance and that there was no way to determine whether they were needy or not.

The problem was that the residents of the Gist Settlements were locked into a dependent relationship with the trustee of Gist's estate. Other African Americans had come to Ohio and created their own lives, but many of the former slaves had been unable to break free of the master-slave relationship they had grown up under. As Philip Schwarz noted, "Gist's will mandated the creation of a trust for the former bondspeople to be managed by a Virginian trustee, a slaveholder himself, and his Ohio agents."[150]

To be sure, some of the freedmen and women left the settlements rather than subject themselves to this form of bureaucratic tyranny. However, doing so meant leaving everything they had gained—their inheritance—behind. And in truth, it wasn't easy. The odds were stacked against free people of color, and not all survived. But Dark Town held on even as the other black settlements disappeared.

A particularly harsh assessment of the settlers was made in 1890 by local historian Daniel Scott:

> *The persons of this race brought to the county were therefore doubtless better than those remaining in slavery, and certainly had decided advantages in the means afforded to better their condition, but it is sad to relate that either from inherent mental weakness or constitutional perversity of disposition, they have failed miserably to meet the expectation of their humanitarian friends. Almost without exception they have squandered the property given them and have sunk in two generations far lower in the scale than those now here who were freed by the general emancipation of 1863.*[151]

Columbus Dispatch reporter Violet Turner provided an update on life in the Highland County Gist Settlement in 1936. "Removed from a state road, in a secluded part of Penn Township in Highland County, is a little world of its own," she wrote.[152] Its seventy residents lived in scattered houses off a winding road. Near the cemetery, the Carthagena Baptist Church and an abandoned school still stood, along with what was the oldest log cabin in the county, if not the state.

Beginning in 1948, parcels of land were sold by the county sheriff to pay back taxes. Although Samuel Turner and some other residents hired an attorney to help them resolve the problem, twenty years later nothing had changed. Although Brown County dealt with the issue of deeds back in 1859, Highland County did not. "Without deeds," reporter Kevin Williams observed, "many families were essentially squatters on their own property. And as people passed away and their homes fell into disrepair, the land sat in limbo."[153]

In 1976, the local newspaper, the *Wilmington News Journal*, wrote of the place, "They are curiously friendly to the visitor. It is a carefree, easy-going community of only eight or nine families."[154] Seventeen years later, Paul Turner, Samuel's grandson, paid $28,000 in delinquent taxes to prevent more plots from being sold off. By then, the original 207-acre tract had shrunk to 161.5 acres.

Dale Robinson is a Gist descendant and Paul's cousin through Hannibal Turner, although they don't see eye to eye on too many things. In the 2013 case of *Turner v. Robinson*, the Highland County Court of Common Pleas decided that Paul was entitled to nineteen of the settlement's thirty-one lots, while Dale was awarded two and part of another. The remainder are lots that are possession of other families that have never acted to obtain clear deeds. However, Paul wants it all because it would have been auctioned off if he hadn't paid the taxes out of his own pocket.

HOCKING COUNTY

Payne's Crossing

PAYNE'S CROSSING (WARD TOWNSHIP)

All that remains of Payne's Crossing is a cemetery south of New Straitsville, tucked away in the Wayne National Forest. In use from 1852 to 1927, it straddles the line separating Hocking (Ward and Green Townships) and Perry Counties (Salt Lick Township). Beginning in the 1830s, Payne's Crossing was an informal community of farms that never gave birth to a village of its own. The earliest settlers—some freedmen and women, others possibly runaway slaves—came to the area from Virginia and bore the surnames Harper, Pointer, Norman, Cross, Harding, Morgan, Gross, Flowers and Lett.[155]

Much of what is known about Payne's Crossing comes from a group of their descendants known as the Old Settlers Reunion. "The original Harpers were among the first settlers of Payne's Crossing in Ohio. The people who lived in the settlement worked in many professions as well as [being] coal miners and farmers. Most had a very light skin tone and may have been children of plantation owners."[156] Census records show that black settlers were initially living with white families and vice versa. Members of the Norman family were concentrated in Green Township and were sometimes referred to as the Norman Settlement. In 1849, Horace Bush married Eliza Flowers, daughter of Nancy Spacey Flowers, in Athens, Ohio. They settled in Ward Township, Hocking County, where Horace owned forty acres of land. It is the easternmost township in Hocking County and includes the unincorporated communities of Murray City, Carbon Hill and Sand Run. Coal Township, Perry County, is to the north. Three years later, at the age of forty-one, Horace registered for the draft. By then, he was living in Michigan.

Since the Paynes apparently did not arrive until the 1860s, the settlement may have originally had another name or, more likely, none at all. Genealogist Sharon Daily traced the ownership of the cemetery: "The initial land was purchased from Jesse and Catharine Payne, who were from Belmont County, in 1859," she said. "Evan, Jesse and Westward Payne, and Amos Robinson bought the land and came here. But the earliest burial was in 1852."[157] One of the men was a druggist and several others were coopers, but most were farmers. Unfortunately, cemetery records are virtually nonexistent. In fact, the 1875 cemetery report for Hocking County dismisses it as "the nigger cemetery."[158]

Jesse and Mary McKee Payne were born free in Prince William County, Virginia. "The Paynes lived in Smith Township in Belmont County. A lot of them were farmers. Jesse and Mary Payne died in Belmont County. Their children moved into the Payne's Crossing area before 1860. Some of them were farmers and others were miners."[159]

There is evidence that the residents of Payne's Crossing provided assistance to fugitive slaves prior to the Civil War, as was true of many black settlements. Some have even suggested that the Underground Railroad was the reason for its existence. However, census records show the settlers were above average in terms of personal wealth, having worked hard, lived frugally and invested wisely. They also kept to themselves because racism was rampant in that region.

Thomas W. Cross was born in Lounden County, Virginia, in 1826. He was the son of a plantation owner named Lee who had come from England. His mother was a slave woman named Cross. "In 1851 at the age of 25, Thomas moved to Hocking County, Ohio. It was said that his father took him there to give him his freedom."[160] The following year, he married Catherine Harper. Altogether they had a dozen children, eight born in Ohio. In 1863, Thomas enlisted in the Union army in Athens, Ohio, serving in the Fifth Regiment of the U.S. Colored Troops with the ambulance detail. Returning home in 1865, he remained a few years before buying a farm in Remus, Michigan. "Because it was inexpensive to buy land he was able to purchase 40 acres for the price of a horse."[161]

In 1867, several Payne's Crossing families left Ohio in covered wagons, John and Sarah Tate and their children among them, and traveled north to Michigan, where they settled in Rolland Township. Born in Pennsylvania,

John had married Sarah A. Guy, daughter of James A. Guy and Deborah Ridgley-Guy. They settled in Hocking County for a while before migrating to Central Michigan.

In the same census, Thomas Harris and his wife, Sarah, were living on their farm with their children Rebecca, Edward, Thomas, Ellen "Elmicy," Ezekiel, Lydia and Amos. A farmhand, Charles Lett, was also staying with them. Thomas moved to Michigan in 1869, taking up residence with his daughter Lydia and her husband, Abner Reed. Ellen married Thomas Squires. Born in (West) Virginia, he had moved to Hocking County. It was there that their daughter Rebecca was born. Not long afterward, they moved to Michigan.

There are five or six graves in Payne's Crossing cemetery believed to contain Civil War veterans. James Betts, Evan Payne and his brother Thomas Payne all served in various Ohio regiments of the U.S. Colored Infantry. However, Henry Striblin, who had a very light complexion, transferred to the Fourth Cavalry Regiment, an all-white outfit. Two of the veterans, Evan Payne and another who has not been identified, served in the Fifth Regiment of the USCT. Dr. Versalle "Verb" Washington, expert on this unit, said that these are the only Fifth USCT markers he knows of outside Arlington Cemetery in Washington, D.C.

The tendency for spouses to be chosen from within the community is illustrated by the marriages of the Civil War veterans. James Betts, who was descended from the slaves freed by Drewry Betts, married Rebecca Harper. The former Betts slaves had settled Captina in Belmont County, Ohio. Evan Payne married Margaret F. "Mary" Norman, while Thomas Payne married Ellen Norman. And Henry Striblen married Ann E. Payne. Although they had seen a bit of the world while serving in the military, all chose to live out their lives in Payne's Crossing. However, there were exceptions. Elijah Lett, for example, took a wife from the Woodson family, the founders of Berlin Crossroads in Jackson County.

Following the Civil War, residents of Payne's Crossing began to move away, some to the cities and others to similar communities. Many of them made their way to central Michigan "in covered wagons drawn by oxen."[162]

Other Old Settler surnames found at Payne's Crossing were Pointer, Norman, Cross, Harding, Morgan, Gross, Flowers and Lett.

Payne's Crossing eventually got caught up in the coal mining boom that spanned 1880 to 1920. The Kramer Brothers Coal Company of New Straitsville, for one, purchased some of the land for its Butterfly mine, and the Copperhead Coal Company of Carbon Hill bought some as well for its Copperhead mine. This contributed to the dissolution of the settlement. As Jim Massie reported, "The last burial occurred in 1927. By that time, most of the family names carved in the sandstone markers—Payne, Striblin, Betts, Harper, Mabry, Lett, Norman, Graison, Dixon and Nixon—had disappeared from the tax and land records of the area."[163]

JACKSON COUNTY

Berlin Crossroads and Ragland Colony

BERLIN CROSSROADS (MILTON TOWNSHIP)

According to the late Minnie S. Woodson, "Family tradition states that Thomas Woodson came to Ohio by way of Greenbrier County, Va. (now West Virginia), an area 100 miles from Jefferson's Monticello home."[164] Thomas, who was black, went to his grave firmly believing that he was the eldest son of President Thomas Jefferson, although there is no documentation linking him to Monticello.[165]

Here is a summation of the Woodson family history as recounted by Minnie:

> *Young Tom told the fact that he was the son of President Thomas Jefferson and Jefferson's dead wife's half-sister* [in other words, Sally Hemings]. *Young Tom had a misunderstanding with his father so he was sent with other slaves to live away from Monticello to John Woodson's farm. When he came of age, he received money from Jefferson or Woodson to buy a farm. Young Tom, who was never a slave, bought the freedom of his wife and children. He took the name Thomas Woodson and went to Ohio to live. He bought a farm and coal was discovered on it. He sold the farm that had coal on it and invested the money in businesses in Pittsburgh.*[166]

The derivation of the Woodson surname hasn't been established, either. Fawn M. Brodie, who wrote several books about Thomas Jefferson, noted that Tarleton and John Woodson were both well-known residents of Albermarle County where Jefferson lived. Thomas possibly lived with one of them and took their surname. However, Minnie Woodson also discovered that Jefferson had an aunt who was married to a Colonel John Woodson.

Thomas and Jemima Riddle Woodson moved with their children to Chillicothe, Ohio, about 1820. An article in the *Colored American* asserted, "Thomas Woodson was the son of his master, and his wife the daughter of hers. He purchased himself and family for $900. He came to this State several years ago, and when he warrived here he was almost penniless."[167] For the next decade, the family remained in Chillicothe.

In those days, African Americans attended white churches, so they joined the local Methodist congregation. However, they were among the first members to break away, forming a black congregation that met in the home of Reverend Peter James. Eventually, it became the Quinn Chapel African Methodist Episcopal Church, the first of forty-four such churches formed by William Paul Quinn and "the first black Methodist church west of the Alleghenies."[168]

In 1830, the Woodsons and eight other black families founded Berlin at a crossroads in nearby Jackson County.[169] Black abolitionist and politician John Mercer Langston was four years old when he and his family passed through the community in 1834. Freed by the terms of their owner's will, they were relocating from Virginia. "When they arrived at Berlin Crossroads…three of the seven travelers had reached their journey's end, deciding to stay at the little settlement where land was cheap and affordable. This was the place to exercise their self-sufficiency now that freedom was theirs."[170]

A correspondent for the *Colored American* visited the community in 1838. Not surprisingly, he came away quite impressed with the Woodsons:

> *He now owns 372 acres of good land, acknowledge to be the best cultivated farm in Jackson county. Sometimes fifty stacks of hay may be seen on his farm in one season. He raises annually from 1500-to-3000 bushels of corn. I have never found a more intelligent, enterprising, farming family in the state of Ohio.*[171]

While Berlin Crossroads was initially a farming community, it had grown to nearly two dozen families, including blacksmiths, carpenters, shoemakers, horsemen, merchants, seamstresses, schoolteachers and clergymen within the span of ten years. It also had two hotels. The wealthiest resident was Thomas Woodson, worth about $13,500. He had also become "a distributing

Quinn Chapel AME Methodist Church in Chillicothe was founded in 1821. *Author photo.*

agent for the *Palladium of Liberty*, an abolitionist newspaper out of Columbus, Ohio, and attended a state convention of blacks in 1844."[172]

The Woodsons emphasized education. Of their eleven children, three became ministers and five educators. Lewis Frederick Woodson, the eldest son, "tutored black children at the Education Benevolent Society in Columbus, Ohio, and later went to Pittsburgh to teach in that city's first black school."[173] Under the pen name "Augustine," he wrote a series of letters for the *Colored American* in the late 1830s and early 1840s that were said to have influenced Martin Delaney, a physician and soldier who is often credited with being the first black nationalist. After becoming a minister, Lewis joined forces with John Vashon, a wealthy black businessman, to found the Pittsburgh Philanthropic Society, which assisted fugitive slaves.

Sarah Jane Woodson was the youngest child of Thomas and Jemima. "In 1852, at age 27, Sarah enrolled in Oberlin College, the first college open to both women and African Americans."[174] Four years later, she completed her bachelor's degree, becoming one of the first black women to graduate from college. Sarah became the first African American college instructor when she was hired to teach English at Wilberforce University in 1858. Two years

Baseball was a popular pastime in many black settlements, starting in the 1860s. *Authors' collection.*

earlier, Sarah's brother, the Reverend Lewis Woodson, had been a founder of the college and one of the original trustees.

In 1868, at the age of forty-two, Sarah married the Reverened Jordan Winston Early, a former slave and a pioneer in the AME Church. For the next twenty years, she supported his ministries, teaching in various schools wherever his preaching took them. It is estimated that by the time she retired in 1888, Sarah had taught more than six thousand children. She then threw her energies into the Woman's Christian Temperance Union (WCTU) and was elected superintendent of the "Colored Division." Five years later, she "was named Representative Woman of the Year at the Chicago World's Fair."[175]

Berlin Crossroads played an important role in the Underground Railroad. "After arriving at Berlin Crossroads, conductors helped the runaways reach the next stop: either Chillicothe or Washington Court House."[176] In a letter to Professor Wilbur Siebert, J.J. Minor recalled, "At Berlin seven miles about Jackson was a settlement of the Stewards, James and Newks and a number of Woodsons. Finely educated people—educated at Oberlin some of them gradually. I think these settlements worked independently."[177] Among those who did their part in assisting the fugitives on their way to freedom were the Nookes, Yancy, Leah, Wilson, Stewart, James, Cassels, Dyer, Brown, Webb, Mundell and Woodson families.

Oral tradition maintains that both Thomas Jr. and John died for their bold defense of their abolitionist principles. Thomas Jr. was allegedly found along the side of the road after sustaining a severe beating to the head from a group of proslavery thugs. He died on September 27, 1846, at the age of thirty-four. Six years later, John was purportedly attacked by a gang of Kentucky slave owners. His life hung in the balance for a year before he succumbed on November 21, 1853, also at the age of thirty-four. Both men were married with children and had died rather than betray runaways. However, like the connection to Thomas Jefferson, these stories have not been substantiated.

By 1870, the best days of Berlin Crossroads were behind it.

RAGLAND COLONY (LIBERTY TOWNSHIP)

William Ragland, an unmarried farmer of Louisa County, Virginia, passed away in 1849, at the age of sixty-nine. In his will dated August 18, 1849, he emancipated his slaves and provided funding—$20,000—for their resettlement in a free state. As was typical of large estates, it took a goodly amount of time to carry out William Ragland's wishes.

Finally, in January 1855, his agent—A.J. Perkins—removed some sixty-eight slaves to Jackson County, Ohio. As he wrote in a letter to the *Jackson Standard*, "Some feeble attempts were made to hinder their settlement; but the intelligent and law abiding citizens of this community discountenanced such a course, and the Negroes were permitted peacefully to occupy the lands purchased for them in this county, with the money provided by their late master."[178]

On her excellent website, genealogist Teresa Vega observed, "All Euro-descended Raglands in the U.S. are related to Evan Ragland."[179] In the mid-1600s, at the age of fourteen, Evan was kidnapped from Somerset, England, and shipped to Virginia, where he became the indentured servant of Stephen Pettus. However, after he had worked off his indenture, he married Pettus's daughter, Susana, and inherited his estate, including some enslaved individuals.

Teresa's research revealed that the Ragland family in Virginia "routinely purchased slaves of Malagasy descent"—in other words, natives of Madagascar.[180] Furthermore, that "African-American Raglands are descendants of children fathered by Ragland men and Malagasy/West African/Native American women and those unrelated enslaved people who took their surname before and after they were emancipated."[181] It is more than likely that William Ragland fathered some of his slaves.[182]

An unusually detailed ledger has survived in which are recorded "the debts and interest charged to each slave by the estate of their former master."[183] The amounts "varied between $2.50 and $330.46"—the last owed by John "for an overcoat, horse, cow and his freedom."[184] In many instances, these costs were paid by others, presumably in exchange for work.

One of William Ragland's former slaves was profiled in a local history. A William Ragland was born to William and Sylvia "Sylvie" Ragland about 1847. "He was emancipated when about two years of age in company with forty-seven others, and came with his mother to Ohio in 1854."[185] After arriving in his new home, he set about acquiring an education and even taught school for several terms. He married Maria Waller, a former slave from Virginia. She had been emancipated by her owner in 1854 and came to Ohio seven years later. William eventually came to own 220 acres of good farmland on a hillside and raised seven children.

While the identity of Maria Waller's former master has not been discovered, the Waller family's association with slavery in Virginia is well known, albeit not always accurately. In Alex Haley's novel *Roots*, the character of Kunta Kinte is purchased at an auction by John Waller of Spotsylvania County. He is then transferred to John's brother, Dr. William "Will" Waller. Although the real-live slave in question was named Toby, Kunta's slave name, the existing records do not coincide with Haley's tale.[186]

It appears that some freedmen may have been drawn to Liberty Township even before the Ragland Colony was founded. In 1877, the *Jackson Standard* provided an account of Nellie Watson, who had purportedly just turned one hundred years old. Born a slave in Louisa County, Virginia, in 1777, she gained her freedom in 1845. The same year, she moved to Ohio and settled in the Ragland Colony on Salt Creek—except the colony did not exist until ten years later. (Perhaps she had actually been born in 1787 and arrived in 1855.) Mrs. Watson was the mother of seven children, four of whom died in Virginia and another in Ohio.

Two of Mary's sons, William and Benjamin, hired themselves out for two years while they were still in Virginia and were able to purchase their father for $500. When they later came to Ohio, he accompanied them and remained with the family for fifteen years. While still enslaved, Nellie joined the Baptist Church. She went on to be a founder and longtime member of the First Baptist Church of Salt Creek.

In 1866, the law firm of Johnson & McClintick published a notice in the Jackson newspaper informing Robert M. Kent, the surviving executor and trustee of Ragland's will, as well as the beneficiaries—the formerly enslaved individuals—that a suit had been filed against them by other claimants. The notice revealed that the executors in the years 1855–60 had "purchased divers tracts or parcels of land in the counties of Pike and Jackson, in the State of Ohio, and…put the said plaintiffs and defendants, as the liberated slaves and legatees of said testator, in the possession and occupation of the same."[187] However, the title to the land was held by Kent, now a resident of Ohio, who had sold some of the land for taxes. As with similar trusteeships, it was a legal nightmare.

In the northwest corner of Liberty Township is Big Rock, a local landmark. A man named Tally Wicker had originally received a patent for the land in 1841. Nathaniel Hill purchased it in 1880 and "in turn, deeded it to John Ragland, Daniel Ragland, and Samuel White."[188] It was here that they founded the Sharon Baptist Church. For many years, "Big Rock Meeting Day" was held at the church, attracting both black and white people from throughout Ohio and adjoining states. It was a homecoming of sorts for the extended Ragland clan.

Perhaps the largest gathering was in 1926, when an estimated two thousand African Americans poured into Liberty Township. However, after 1962–63, the annual Big Rock Meeting Day celebration appears to have died out, and now not even the church remains.

JEFFERSON COUNTY

McIntyre Settlement or Hayti

MCINTYRE COLORED SETTLEMENT OR HAYTI
(WAYNE TOWNSHIP)

In the early years of the nineteenth century, Ohio became the locus of activity for the Society of Friends. By 1800, some eight hundred Quaker families were living within the Ohio Country; by 1826, there were more than eight thousand Quakers in just four eastern counties of the state: Belmont, Harrison, Columbiana and Jefferson.

Mount Pleasant, a Quaker village in Jefferson County, became a hub for the antislavery movement. Nathan Updegraff, a leader of the local Quakers, was a delegate to the first Ohio constitutional convention. Not only did he staunchly oppose permitting slavery within the state, but he also voted to extend various civil rights, including the right to vote, to black people. It is not surprising, then, that people of color—freed or otherwise—would be drawn to Jefferson County as well.

Abraham G. Naylor, the son of strict Quakers, had been a slaveholder in Maryland, but "on coming to Ohio set them free."[189] It is not clear whether Naylor manumitted his slaves before or after he came to Ohio in 1812 and settled in the Quaker community of Smithfield, Jefferson County. However, the 1830 census shows a Richard Naylor of Mount Pleasant heading a household consisting of three other free persons of color.

Concord Hicksite meetinghouse was the locus of early Quaker activity in Ohio. *Author photo.*

Whether Naylor provided his manumitted slaves with assistance is unknown, but Nathaniel Benford did. There are two detailed accounts of the black settlement known either as McIntyre Colored Settlement or Hayti (sometimes Haiti), though it had no official name. Both tell pretty much the same story, but they do diverge on certain points, primarily when it comes to names. For example, who was McIntyre? Either he was a man who had been killed by Indians along the stream that bears his name or he was the man who was entrusted with conveying the former slaves from Virginia to Ohio.

In 1825, Nathaniel Benford, a slave owner of Charles City County, Virginia, freed seven of his slaves.[190] Because they could not remain in Virginia without risk of being re-enslaved, he sent them to a friend, Benjamin Ladd, in Smithfield Township. Originally from Virginia, Ladd came to Ohio in 1814. After purchasing a farm known as Prospect Hill from his father-in-law, he began a meatpacking business, curing and packing pork and bacon, sending the meat back east to Richmond, Virginia.

Like many men in the region, Ladd was a Quaker, an abolitionist and a leading member of the Orthodox Society of Friends. Ladd placed the former slaves on some property along Stillwater Creek in Harrison County. But they did not remain there long. Farmers in the vicinity soon began hiring them away, and the so-called Stillwater Settlement quickly collapsed.[191]

The Mount Pleasant home of pioneering antislavery newspaper publisher Benjamin Lundy. *Author photo.*

Benford had been inspired to liberate his slaves by the example of a neighbor, David Minge, who had freed eighty-seven of his own and sent them to live in Cuba. Certainly, Benford's first effort had not turned out quite the way he had envisioned. Nevertheless, he made a second attempt in 1829. After drawing up manumission papers for nine families of slaves from his plantation, W.H. Hunter related, he transported them to Smithfield and again turned them over to Benjamin Ladd. This time, his instructions were more explicit.

Ladd purchased 260 acres from Thomas Mansfield in Wayne Township, about two miles from Smithfield. With the money Benford had given him, Ladd was able to erect cabins and buy the necessary implements to farm the land. "The heads of the original families were: Nathaniel ['Nattie'] Benford, who took the name of his master; Ben Messenburg, Collier Christian, Lee Carter, Paige Benford, David Cooper, William Toney, Fielding Christian and Fitzhugh Washington."[192]

Judge Mansfield's account differs somewhat from that of Hunter. For one thing, Mansfield suggested that there were thirty or forty families altogether. He also identified the slave owner as Thomas Beaufort. "The families," Powell wrote, "were the married sons and daughters of Nathaniel Beaufort who had been his master's 'nigger driver,' was the way one of his granddaughters put it. The whole colony was under Nathaniel Beaufort's control as long as he lived, during which time it prospered."[193]

The former slaves were conveyed to Ohio and located on the property by "McIntyre," who returned to Virginia within a few days. "He was never in the community again, nor was any other representative of the Beaufort's so far as anybody knows."[194] The land was divided up into five-acre plots, with a cabin on each plot to house a particular family. Mansfield did not believe that the land was ever recorded in the names of the former slaves but rather deeded to Benjamin Ladd as trustee.

No doubt due to his closeness to their former master, "Nattie" emerged as the leader of the colony. He also had the largest family and received the most property, which had been divided into parcels of three to fifteen acres, based on the number of children. It is believed that he married a woman named Allie Carter and had fourteen children. His brother, Levie Benford, purportedly married a white Quaker woman named Mary Cordell. The colonists, Hunter claimed, placed considerable emphasis on kinship, acknowledging blood ties as distant as a forty-sixth cousin. "That they are all related some way is probably a fact, as they have been very exclusive in their alliances with families of color outside the settlement." Some of the lighter skinned members suggested that their paternity could be traced back "to some of the first families in Virginia."[195]

The former slaves became well known to their neighbors due to their various talents. Benny Messenburg was consulted by many for his expertise at growing things. Carter Christian was a highly praised cook. Lee Carter was the longtime porter at the "Old Black Bear" in Steubenville, where he regaled visitors with his entertaining stories. "Old Fielding" was much in demand when it came time for butchering. And Evens Benford acquired a reputation as a huckster.

However, unlike Benford's first seven slaves, the colonists of Hayti were determined to remain on their land and live off the proceeds. First, they had to clear it, most of it being woodlands. Next, they planted the crops they knew from Virginia—tobacco, flax, hemp—but these were hard on the soil. So they turned to corn, oats, rye and various garden vegetables, the latter tended by the women. It was a constant battle against "red brush and rank weeds"—a battle they eventually lost.[196] Their critics blamed it on their laziness, pointing out that the surrounding farms were thriving. But it was also acknowledged that their farming experience had been gained in "the richest land in the valley of the James river."[197] They knew nothing about soil conservation or the need for fertilization.

"Whether they had any teams and money to start with," C.A. Powell wrote, "it is not known to Judge Mansfield, but he thought that they did not. Both men and women had to 'work out' much of the time for means to go upon, the girls toiling as servants in the community for twenty-five to fifty cents per week and their keep, the men receiving forty to fifty cents per day often paid in such provisions as meal and meat."[198]

Hunter asserted that Ladd worked very closely with the black colonists, assisting them however he could. "It was not his fault, and it was not the fault of Mr. Benford that the negroes deteriorated after being freed and given opportunity to labor for themselves. They were given every possible chance—there was nothing wanting outside individual energy and faculty to make successful this philanthropic endeavor."[199] Seventy-five years after the colony's founding, Judge Mansfield did not feel that its financial or physical condition was any better than it had been at the start.

To their credit, the residents of Hayti were well behaved in the view of Judge Mansfield. He attributed this to their being regular churchgoers, attending either the Methodist or the Baptist church, each having a black preacher. The one exception was "Lucy Cardwell [Carter], who in practice and in principle was a Quaker, and whose piety and patience under long suffering were made the subject of a long Abolition tract written by Elizabeth Ladd."[200]

Hunter was impressed with the fervor of their religious practices, if not the authority of their beliefs. "Although many of the original settlers had very little knowledge of the Bible, what they did know was to them during these meetings, 'like honey and the honey-comb.'"[201] The congregation would become so overwhelmed in their religious ecstasy that some fell into a trance for hours a time, while other began dancing wildly until the whole church was caught up in "religious pandemonium."[202]

As of 1879, there were approximately fifty or sixty African Americans still residing on the land, representing eleven families. The original settlers were fine physical specimens, "as fine," Judge Mansfield declared, "as the community ever saw."[203] However, by the end of the nineteenth century, their cabins were

in a miserable condition. The land once so fertile and admirably situated for abundant crops is now for the most part stony and sterile. Scarcely any care has been taken to improve it and almost every portion is so overgrown with brush and weeds that it would now be impossible to improve it. The descendants of the original settlers manage to eke out an existence upon it and that is all.[204]

Angela Feenerty, president of the Mount Pleasant Historical Society, has delved into the story of the former Taliaferro (or Talliafero) slaves. In 1855, Ann W. "Nancy" Taliaferro of King William County, Virginia, passed away. She owned a well-known farm called Warsaw near the village of Aylett. By the terms of her will, all of her slaves were to be emancipated and provided with $150 apiece to facilitate their relocation to a free state. "Initially they intended to take them to Kansas but thought better of it and decided to take them to Mount Pleasant to settle them among the Quakers," Feenerty noted.[205]

When they boarded the train for Ohio, the "colored persons" numbered about two dozen, according to witnesses. "They were brought up with much care by the deceased lady, and are represented by the executor to be both intelligent and possessed of good morals."[206] The *Wheeling Times* put their number at about thirty when the group passed through (West) Virginia en route to Mount Pleasant.[207] "The difference in numbers may be because some of the slaves Nancy Talliafero freed were held back by a lawsuit," Feenerty suggested.[208]

The *Richmond Dispatch* reported that F.W. Scott, the executor of the estate, visited the former slaves in May 1857. He purportedly "found them in a wretched condition, almost starving. One of the children had been stolen, and several had died for the want of attention and the necessaries of life. They begged Mr. S. to allow them to return with him to Virginia and go into slavery."[209]

By 1935, the *Steubenville Herald Star* stated there were forty former slaves altogether, including "Charlotte Pollard Hargrave, Onea Baxter Walker, Harriet Lawson Wooten, Thomas Robinson and Ottawa Moore."[210] Feenerty has identified possibly twenty more, mostly children.

LAWRENCE COUNTY

Blackfork, Burlington and Ironton

BLACKFORK SETTLEMENT (WASHINGTON TOWNSHIP)

At the beginning of the nineteenth century, a few pioneering industrialists were already being lured to Lawrence County by its natural resources. Salt, coal, clay, iron, timber—and, later, oil and gas—were present in abundance. But that was the rub. There were more jobs—and good-paying jobs at that—than there were takers.

Located along Black Fork branch of Symmes Creek in Washington Township, Blackfork was largely founded by people of color, possibly including some American Indians. Just a few miles south of Oak Hill, it likely began as a farm community, but in time expanded to include ironmaking and, finally, brickmaking.

The earliest mention of Blackfork was about 1818, when twenty freed slaves from Poke Patch, three miles to the southwest, are said to have organized the Union Baptist Church. A year later, the worshippers built a log structure on the farm of Dicky Jones and installed Reverend K.L. Carter of Franklin Valley, Jackson County, as the first minister. In 1879, a new church was constructed on the John Keels farm using lumber salvaged from an earlier church. Forty years after that, it was replaced by a wooden frame building on Niner Hill Road. Having survived for two centuries, Union Baptist Church is the oldest active African American Baptist church in Ohio.

According to a Lawrence County atlas, "At one time part of the Hanging Rock Iron Region, Olive, Pioneer, and Washington iron furnaces, operated within the township."[211] Situated on the banks of Olive Creek, Olive Furnace was built in 1846. Washington Furnace, on Black Fork Creek, followed in 1853 and Pioneer Furnace on Brady Creek four years after that. Each one would have required about one hundred workers to operate, and they generally would have lived on site or close by.

The demand for labor could not be satisfied by the white settlers alone. The working conditions were dangerous and backbreaking, so the door was thrown open to people of color by furnace owner John Campbell and others. As a result, Blackfork became a destination for African Americans, including fugitive slaves. In fact, Campbell was active in the Ironton network of the Underground Railroad, concealing runaways in his twenty-two-room mansion.

In 2008, a team of Ohio University students spent spring quarter interviewing residents of Blackfork. "What the students found was an area in northern Lawrence County where African Americans, Native Americans and Euro Americans lived and worked in the 1800s," David Melloy reported. "When the iron, clay and brick industries moved into the area, the

The ruins of historic Olive Furnace, which once spawned a company town. *Author photo.*

multicultural workers in Blackfork worked alongside each other and were paid the same at a time when most other areas of the country separated races and cultures."[212]

Several cemeteries bear witness to Black Fork's history—Washington Furnace, Union Baptist Church and Bethel. However, by the beginning of the twentieth century, most of the resources had been depleted and the jobs had disappeared. Surnames once found in Blackfork included Baker, Beverly, Brown, Chavous, Davis, Harris, Howard and Rickman.

BURLINGTON (FAYETTE TOWNSHIP)

John Ward Jr. passed away on October 11, 1826, in Sulfur Springs (now Gretna), Pittsylvania County, Virginia, at the age of seventy-nine. An unmarried planter, Ward left a will dated July 31, 1826, in which he bequeathed sums of money and property (including his interest in a toll bridge) to various friends and relatives. He was, he avowed, "in a low state of health but of sound mind and disposing memory."[213] And he did not forget his slaves.

"It is my will and desire," Ward wrote, "that all of my slaves now living or which may be living at the time of my death be free and I do herby bequeath to each and everyone of them their freedom immediately upon my death in as full an unlimited manner as the laws of Virginia will admit of."[214] To David "Davy" Ward and his sister, Nancy, whom he described as "fireside servants," he specified that each would receive $150, a horse worth $40 and two cows. To Will, Sam, Ned and Ben—four elderly slaves—he gave a piece of land. And to "all my slaves over 15 years of age at the time of my death each the sum of $20."[215]

Numbering seventy in all, the manumitted slaves arrived in Lawrence County the following year. Although they had "little or no property of value" and many of them were "ragged and dirty," all of them quickly found places to live.[216] Some of them had even "obtained security as the law requires"— that is to say, they posted a bond to ensure their good behavior—"and probably the balance will within twenty days."[217]

At least some of the manumitted slaves retained the Ward surname. For example, in 1827, David Ward petitioned to remain in Pittsylvania County following his emancipation. In doing so, he stated that he had attended his master—"John Ward the elder"—during his illness and that he had "he never slept out of his master's room, for twenty five years of his life."[218]

Some of Ward's former slaves likely gravitated to the black communities such as Burlington, Getaway, Blackfork and Poke Patch. In 1840, Harry Ward was the head of a "free colored" household that consisted of six people in Fayette Township, or Burlington. Other free black households in Fayette Township included Essex Harris (seven), Gam Bland (three), William Bryant (five), William Reed (six), Jones Craddock (two), Letty Calloway (one), Betry Burton (four), Jack Miller (five), Camillers Hall (three), Pleasant Roberts (ten), James Pigman (one), Johnathan Bryant (three), George Bryant (three), Robert Bradfield (two), Timothy Harris (six), Philo Lynch (three), Mary Fraddolka (six), Abner Broon (four), Charles Roberts (three) and Emila Shephard (seven).

James Twyman, a planter in Madison County Virginia, was a sixty-eight-year-old bachelor when he passed away in February 1849. In his will, he provided that his thirty-seven slaves would be set free. Because three of his most faithful servants—Noah, Winney and Joe—were elderly and infirm, he stipulated that they would be looked after as long as they continued in live in Madison County. Three others who were considered his favorites—Jenny, Amanda and Frances Ann—were provided with enough funds to meet their anticipated needs: $18,000 (or about $500,000 in today's dollars). Amanda and Frances Ann—Jenny's daughter and granddaughter, respectively—were also each given $800 in cash (about $22,000 apiece).

Finally, Twyman bequeathed them "all my silver plate, my clock and watch, my household furniture of every description, two good horses, four good milk cows, all my fowls…and plentiful supply of provisions for [the livestock]…and all the hay, straw and long food which may be and remains on the land [that is given] to them…" some 200 acres.[219] As for the remaining thirty-seven, he left them $10,000 (or approximately $330,000 in today's dollars), as well as clothing, livestock and various farming implements.

Predictably, the will was contested, but Twyman's relatives ultimately lost. However, they had one final card to play. In a final expression of their contempt, they denied James Twyman burial in the family cemetery.

The group that left Madison is believed to have numbered thirty. "Entering Lawrence County, OH, across the river from what today is Huntington, WV, the group by that time numbered 31, an aptly named infant—William Traveler Smith—having arrived en route."[220] The former slaves had traveled some four hundred miles to Burlington. Arriving in October 1849, they purchased 640 acres of land from a man named Isaac Frampton for $6,000—they referred to their new home as the "Promised Land." The property included one large frame house and several small tenant houses.

The Burlington 37, as they came to be called, consisted of twenty men and seventeen women. "Some of them were old men and women, who had given the best part of their lives in toil for their master, in the accursed bond of slavery," John G. Wilson later wrote.[221] By 1850, Noah, one of the three servants for whom special provision had been made, arrived in Ohio, using the surname Twyman. However, several others returned to Virginia after the Civil War.

Originally the county seat of Lawrence County, Burlington was founded in 1817, taking its name from the town in Vermont. It was directly opposite the mouth of (West) Virginia's Big Sandy River. The Twyman slaves joined the existing Baptist church. "Organized in 1807 and established in 1813, it was built on Charley Creek Hill two miles north of Burlington, and was reached by means of a trail that led up the hill."[222]

Together with their white neighbors, they transported lumber across the Ohio River to build a church on Macedonia Ridge—a one room, twenty-by-thirty-foot, wood-frame structure. Martha Kouns noted, "Eli Thayer of Massachusetts was an abolitionist congressman and founder of Ceredo, [West Virginia], who supplied lumber for the church."[223] They called it the Macedonia Missionary Baptist Church.

A memorial to the Burlington 37 has been erected in a South Point Cemetery. *Author photo.*

Macedonia Missionary Baptist Church is the "Mother Church" for eight others in Ohio. *Author photo.*

According to the 1859 census, when the former Twyman slaves came to Lawrence County, they formed five households.[224] The surnames were mostly Twyman but also Fry and Toms. The last consisted of seventeen people. Given the size of the Toms household, there was undoubtedly pressure on the children to move out as soon as they could fend for themselves. For the young women, this meant they should find husbands. They married men with surnames Jackson, Killgore, King and Shelton.

Largely through the efforts of Owen Pleasant, who counts a Twyman among his ancestors, the Thirty-Seven Cemetery was spruced up and a monument with the words "Promised Land" was erected to the original settlers. Macedonia is recognized as the original mother church to many other black Baptist churches.

IRONTON (UPPER TOWNSHIP)

In 1856, Dr. Peter C. Holt and his wife, Susannah, moved to Ohio from Kentucky so that he could emancipate their slaves, over thirty in number. The son of Thomas and Charlotte Blackburn Holt, Peter was born near Petersburg, Virginia, in 1782, but moved to Bardstown, Kentucky, seven years later with his parents. He received his education under the guidance of Reverend Joshua L. Wilson, DD, which included the study of medicine. Settling down on a farm in Union County, Kentucky, Peter, a physician by training, acquired the title "Judge."

Childless, Peter became the patron of his nephew, J.F. Given, who graduated from Marietta College in 1847. Although Peter was a "practical abolitionist," Reverend Given followed a different track entirely.[225] He had quickly risen to prominence in the Ohio Conference of the Methodist Church but proved to be so "intensely proslavery" that he was "charged with disloyalty by his brethren of the church."[226] As editor of the *Christian Witness*, Givens became the mouthpiece for "the copperhead church movement" and a "stump-speaker" for Clement Vallandigham, an antiwar Democrat from Ohio who was convicted of treason.[227]

Nevertheless, it was under the influence of his nephew, who preached at Spencer Chapter, that Holt came to Ironton. At the age of seventy-five or so, Holt decided he wanted to dispose of his farm and free his slaves. Newspapers reported, "He removed to Ironton himself, and spent the remainder of his days in superintending the freedom of those who had been his slaves—buying small farms for some, and establishing others in business to which they were suited."[228] In 1860, two "mulatto" girls—Alice Housen, age fifteen, and Velina Housen, age seven—were living in his household. And at least ten of the manumitted slaves had taken the Holt surname. Other surnames were Black, Gibson, Harris, Hett, Housen, Rager and Vinov.

Albert Holt, who died in 1888, was one of Peter's slaves. In Albert's obituary, it is noted that while Judge Holt was living, he "exercised toward them a most fatherly care. He bought a little farm above Ice Creek for one of them. He, also, purchased the cottage where Mrs. Moreland lives for another, and it has remained in the family of the owner ever since."[229] When Peter Holt passed away in March 1861, a month before the start of the Civil War, he was said to have been greatly mourned by his former slaves.

Many fugitives were guided to Poke Patch from Ironton. Founded by John Campbell in 1849, Ironton was named after the region's most prominent industry and took its street names from various furnaces. During his career, Campbell worked in fourteen furnaces, built eleven and held an interest in eight. Like his good friend John Rankin, he was also a well-known

John Campbell's "Old Hecla" was once the most famous blast furnace in the country. *Authors' collection.*

John Campbell was an iron maker, underground railroader and the founder of Ironton. *Authors' collection.*

abolitionist. Owing to his views on slavery, Campbell left the Democratic Party in 1848. In the following years, he cofounded the Ohio Iron & Coal Company, becoming its first president. In this capacity, he orchestrated the purchase of four hundred acres of land and platted the town of Ironton, which he also named.[230]

Gabrial N. "Gabe" Johnson, an African American conductor of the Underground Railroad, recalled making his first visit to the area of Ironton in 1848, when there were fewer than fifteen houses. According to Johnson, he worked closely with Campbell, traveling "those woods together when the snow was [a] foot deep."[231] Originally from Ripley, Campbell moved to the Hanging Rock Region in 1834, at the age of twenty-six. He quickly became involved in budding iron industry, building on the work of John Means and his son, Thomas. According to LaRoche, research "indicates that profits from prosperous iron furnace industry in the Hanging Rock Iron Region were used to subsidize the Underground Railroad in the area, supplying horses, saddles, and wagons."[232]

LOGAN COUNTY

Five Colonies

MARMON VALLEY (JEFFERSON TOWNSHIP)

The Marmon brothers—Robert, Martin and Samuel—settled in Jefferson Township about 1805. They were from North Carolina, and the area in which they took up residence, not far from Zanesfield, would come to be known as the Marmon Valley. Among the other early black settlers in Jefferson Township were John Newsom and Kinchen Artes, "followed by Tabarns, Byrds, Wades, Waldens, Stewarts, Allens, Ashes, Madrys, Marnings and others, until, from 1840 to 1850, they constituted a very considerable element in the population of the township."[233]

The Newsoms were held in high regard. Henry Newsom had also come from North Carolina and purchased 105 acres from Robert Marmon. His grandson Darius Newsom became a leading teacher in the black schools of the county.

Largely populated by Quakers, Jefferson Township was a safe haven for African Americans. "Many of them have acquired a considerable amount of property and become good, intelligent citizens," a historian noted, "while others, less energetic and provident, have made little or no advancement."[234] However, by 1880, the number of black families in Jefferson Township had declined to one. Perhaps, it had been no more than "an attractive stopping-place by an oppressed race."[235]

Warwick Colony (Stokes Township)

Not much is known about the Warwick Colony. The story begins when Captain John M. Warwick, a resident of Amherst County, Virginia, "conceived the humane idea of giving his colored people their freedom, and establishing them upon lands he should buy for them."[236] A wealthy slave owner, he was in "feeble health, but of sound mind" when he drew up his will, which he signed on February 23, 1848. In it, he stated:

> *The future condition of my Slaves has long been an anxious concern with me, and it is my deliberate intention, wish and desire, that the whole of them be manumitted and set free as soon after my demise as the growing crops shall be saved, and the annual hires terminated—not later than the end of year of my death—to be removed, or so many of them as I do not manumit and send to a Free State during my life, with the exception hereinafter named to, and settled in one or more of the Free States of this Union, under the care and direction of my Executors hereinafter appointed. Indiana is my choice.*[237]

The elderly tobacco planter made special provision for his "faithful and confidential servant, Frederick, and his wife, Lucy, and her eight children; also my cook, Nicey, and her three youngest children, as well as any others hereafter born in either family."[238] He wanted them to be able to continue to live for the rest of their lives in the homes that had been occupying on his plantation. Frederick was, he noted, "very infirm, and his family a helpless one."[239]

After any outstanding debts were satisfied and the charges of administering his estate were paid, Warwick wanted the slaves to receive the remainder of his wealth to cover the cost of "their comfortable clothing, outfit, travelling expenses and settlements in their new homes, with such provision for their comfort, sustenance and support afterwards, as the fund will provide."[240] Toward that end, Warwick appointed Dr. David Patterson of Amherst County and two others as his executors, expecting full well that Patterson would perform most of the duties.

On March 17, 1848, Warwick died. His will was probated three days later. The *Anti-Slavery Bugle* and other newspapers soon reported that Warwick "manumitted by his will all his servants, numbering between 70 and 80. He has made ample provision for their removal, outfit and settlement in one of the Western States."[241] However, the official count appended to Warwick's will was seventy-five.

Most bequests of this sort took time, as various legal objections and challenges were filed. But the biggest problem was one Warwick had not anticipated. "Before arrangements for their [the slaves'] removal to Indiana could be perfected, that state adopted its constitution of 1851, whereby free negroes and mulattoes were inhibited from coming into the state."[242] Presumably, Patterson had been hard at work on the Indiana plan and now had to start over, further delaying the slaves' emancipation.

Consequently, Patterson traveled to the vicinity of Stokes Township, Logan County, Ohio, and purchased a large tract of land. "During the years 1851–52, the colony, numbering nearly three hundred, arrived and began settlement."[243] Despite Warwick's special provision for them, Frederick and Nicey elected to accompany the others to Ohio. By the terms of the will, the formerly enslaved individuals were to be provided with cabins, various provisions and whatever else they might need to sustain them for as long as the money held out. However, Patterson had not spent the money wisely. Perhaps, when the Indiana deal fell through, he felt pressured to move quickly and was not as prudent as he should have been.

Even as the freedmen and women were settling in, construction had begun on Lewistown Reservoir—or Indian Lake, as it would later be called. Designed as a feeder lake for the Miami and Erie canal system, it was largely

Nothing remains of the Warwick Colony except a few graves in Ghormley Cemetery. *Author photo.*

formed by creating a dam that soon flooded the lowlands. Much of this property belonged to the Warwick Colony. Finding themselves residing on the edge of a swamp, the former slaves were stricken with malaria, and one-sixth of their number died. As Mingo Banks, a colony member, later recalled, they "begin to move out purty lively."[244] They sold what they could and abandoned the rest. Only one of them, Richard Thomas, still remained in Stokes Township thirty years later. Others had scattered throughout Logan County and elsewhere.

The Warwick colonists consisted of eleven families and one group who had no families. Frederick and Nicey's family apparently retained the name Warwick (or Warnick). Frederick's son, Richard T. Warwick, stayed in the area and is buried in Ghormley Cemetery, Lakeview, Logan County. Lot and Clara, who stayed in Logan County, appear to have adopted the name Hampton for some reason. Caleb, Fayette, and "Dingo" (Mingo) were members of the Banks family. The surnames Brown and Dean may have also been used by the colonists.

Flat Woods (Bokescreek Township)

While attending the Ohio constitutional convention of 1850–51, Benjamin Staunton implored his fellow delegates "to authorize the General Assembly to pass an act providing for the extradition of the black population of Ohio."[245] He was speaking on behalf of the citizens of Logan and Hardin Counties who had become increasingly alarmed by the growing number of African Americans who were settling in that region of the state.

Many people of color had come to Logan County, in particular, but not all remained. "Before this time," a local historian later wrote, "the colored people had begun to leave in considerable numbers, going at first to Mercer County, about the time of the building of the Saint Mary's reservoir, and later to Cass County, Mich., and more recently still to Paulding County."[246] However, there were still a few colonizations on the horizon.

In the southwest part of Bokescreek Township, there was a large black settlement called Flat Woods. The first African American to settle there was Christopher Williams, who arrived in 1854 from Fayette County, Ohio, although he had been born in Virginia. Within ten years, the settlers had built a schoolhouse. "A Baptist meeting house was erected about the same time; this was a log building," according to a county history.[247]

In the 1860 census, there were only two black families listed: Newsom and Teig. However, by 1870, there were eighteen different surnames: Austin, Bowser, Bramblet, Burwill, Denney, Hathcock, Hays, Hews, Holland, Jand, Leag, McGinnis, Perry, Peel, Russell, Scott, Stewart and Williams. "This settlement is noted for its camp-meetings and revivals," wrote a historian in 1880.[248]

NEWLIN COLONY (RUSHCREEK TOWNSHIP)

John Newlin became a slave owner for the express purpose of freeing them. A "merchant, industrialist, land speculator, abolitionist, and Quaker leader, [John] was born in the southeastern part of present-day Alamance County [North Carolina]."[249] He used only hired workers in his many successful enterprises and was an outspoken opponent of slavery. John was also an active member of the Manumission Society of North Carolina, assisting slave owners in liberating their slaves. Usually, this involved a lot of legal wrangling because of North Carolina's laws governing such matters.

When her first husband died, Sarah Foust Freeman inherited twenty-five to forty slaves. Although they had discussed freeing them, her late husband had never gotten around to doing so. Before she entered into a second marriage, "she and her prospective husband signed an agreement that left her in complete control of her slaves and other property."[250] After she remarried, Sarah revised her will to leave her slaves to John Newlin, having previously arranged with him to take them to a free state and give them their freedom.

However, when Sarah passed away in 1839, a number of would-be heirs stepped forward and filed a blizzard of lawsuits in an attempt to break the will and claim the slaves. Three of the lawsuits eventually made their way to the North Carolina Supreme Court, the last in 1851. During the ensuing twelve years, John had been prevented from acting upon Sarah's wishes. He also, apparently, put the slaves to work in order to pay for their own upkeep, but there is no evidence that he personally profited from their labor.

Finally, the court ruled in John's favor, and he was able to remove the slaves to Logan County where "from motives of benevolence and humanity have manumitted and set free from slavery and bonds of servitude"—forty-two in all.[251] Most went by the surname Newlin, but a few adopted Burnett,

Carter and Nichols. The Newlins did not make a good impression. "They were directly from a state of slavery," the author of a county history wrote in 1880, "having been manumitted by their master by will. As a class, they were much inferior to the colored people hitherto in the country, being sadly addicted to the use of intoxicating drinks."[252]

This rather harsh assessment is borne out by a series of newspaper articles chronicling their criminal behavior, which culminated in the lynching of Seymour Newlin. (It may have been a case of mistaken identity.)[253] However, by 1900, there were Newlins in Rushcreek, Monroe, Perry and Brokencreek Townships in Logan County.

MENDENHALL SETTLEMENT (MONROE TOWNSHIP)

A Quaker by birth, George C. Mendenhall was a prominent attorney in Guilford County, North Carolina. Although he was personally opposed to slavery, he married a young woman named Eliza Webb Dunn in 1824, just as she was "coming into an inheritance of several thousand acres of land and 24 slaves."[254] As a result, he was immediately disowned by the Deep River Meeting of Friends. Two years later, his wife died in childbirth, and the slaves became his problem.

The trouble was that North Carolina law prohibited releasing slaves within the state. Neither could they be freed by will. The only option was to ship them to a free state and emancipate them there. So George did nothing. Well, not quite. He did see to it that all of his slaves received specialized training. "On his farm the negroes were trained as special workmen; carpentry, harnessmaking, shoemaking, tailoring, cooking, agriculture, reached a high state of perfection," one historian wrote. "The problem of the education of the negro was solved."[255]

George's second wife, Delphinia E. Gardner, was a devout Quaker who supported her husband's desire to emancipate the slaves. In order to gain her mother's consent to their marriage, George had made a declaration that he would "liberate [the slaves] as rapidly as he could settle them comfortably upon the free soil of Ohio."[256] But he didn't, at least not right away. While he never sold one, he did purchase family members who had become separated in order to keep them together. Consequently, his slave holdings increased until at one point he claimed that he had seventy altogether. (His brother put the figure at close to one hundred.)

Finally, George put his long-delayed plan into effect. On June 15, 1854, he executed a power of attorney authorizing Willis (or Willie) White ("my Black Boy") to transport Huldah (daughter of Willis and Sarah) and Nebo Gaunt, two of his slaves, to Ohio. They were expected to leave for Ohio early in September in company with a Samuel White and others who were traveling to Indiana. George suggested that Huldah and Nebo might be left in Chillicothe or some neighboring town or county but that they were to ultimately reach Logan County where they would be cared for by Quakers Joshua Marmon and Asa Williams.

Four days later, George added a third slave, Columbus, the six-year-old son of Mahala (Huldah's cousin) to this party. Columbus had been badly burned when his clothes caught fire and bore scars on his body and face. A letter reveals that George was secretly planning to include even more slaves but did not want word of it to get out, likely because he feared backlash from his neighbors. In fact, he sent nine of them to Ohio on July 11, 1854.

George had purchased a two-horse wagon for the journey and hired John White, a former deputy sheriff, to oversee the operation. He, in turn, hired a young man named Felix Frazer to assist. "I have nothing to leave for our colored folks there," George wrote, "they can all earn their own living & that of their children with proper management."[257] As a postscript, George noted that the freed slaves—thirteen in all—had adopted the surname Mendenhall.

On June 28, 1855, George presented a deed of emancipation for twenty-eight formerly enslaved individuals to the clerk of courts in Logan County, Ohio. In doing so, he declared that his action was "in consideration of his own views and of the proper construction of the Declaration of Independence."[258] They represented three families, one led by Willis, one by Dolly and the last by Mahala.

Eventually, George Mendenhall intended to manumit all of his slaves. But on March 9, 1860, while returning home from Stanly County Superior Court, George attempted to drive his buggy across the rain-swollen Uwharie River. The next day, his body and was found "when someone noticed the horse and wheels of the buggy."[259] The onus was now upon his widow to free the remaining slaves.

In May 1861, Delphinia arranged for John Hiatt to transport a small party of slaves to Ohio. But the "group was turned back by an angry mob at Kernersville [North Carolina] and returned to Jamestown."[260] Apparently, the intrepid widow had accompanied them on the trip, for years later she recalled the incident in a letter: "In 1861 I started with all the remainder, & was turned back by an armed mob—There was great rejoicing among the

Delphinia Mendenhall had to entrust her slaves to a Union officer. *Authors' collection.*

pro-slavery part of the community."[261] Delphinia waited more than three years before trying again. In November 1864, "having obtained permission from local authorities, she herself took nine of the remaining slaves as far as Norfolk, Va., where she was told by Union authorities that if she passed through the lines she couldn't return."[262]

A Union officer volunteered to take custody of the slaves and see to it they reached Ohio. Given one hour to consider the proposal, Delphinia decided she could trust this stranger and gave him some gold to cover the travel expenses. Years later, she learned that the officer had been as good as his word. As of the 1860 census, there was but one family of freed Mendenhalls in Logan County and another group in Morrow County. Ten years later, they had spread to Champaign, Delaware and Washington Counties as well, no doubt in search of opportunity, including spouses.

MERCER COUNTY

Carthagena

CARTHAGENA (MARION TOWNSHIP)

Of all free black settlements in Ohio prior to the Civil War, Carthagena in Mercer County was said to be the largest—perhaps the largest in any state. Like nearly all of them, little evidence remains of this once bustling community, save for a cemetery, which held 240 headstones as of 1952. The last person to be buried there was Albert Bowles, who passed away on March 30, 1957, at the age of fifty.

Architectural historian Mary Ann Brown wrote that the settlement of Carthagena "was about ten miles south of Celina and Grand Lake St. Marys at the intersection of State Route 127 and State Route 274. Blacks were apparently in the county before the Shawnee Indians had been removed from Wapakoneta in 1832."[263]

Today, Carthagena is an unincorporated area of Marion Township, dominated by St. Aloysius Catholic Church and St. Charles Seminary. As early as 1856, German Catholic settlers began purchasing large tracts of land from the original black owners. Eventually, white men bought it all and established their own cemetery, separated from the existing black one by a wrought-iron fence.

For years, free blacks and runaway slaves had been making their way to Ohio, many gravitating to Cincinnati because of its location directly across the Ohio River from the slave state of Kentucky and the availability of

Carthagena's black cemetery stands in the shadow of Saint Aloysius Roman Catholic Church. *Author photo.*

work on the waterfront. However, for two weeks in August 1829, African Americans in Cincinnati clashed with lawless bands of Irish immigrants with whom they were in competition for jobs. Perhaps 1,200 or more were driven out of the city, some finding refuge in Canada. In the aftermath, an uneasy truce existed between the races.

During the winter of 1833–34, Augustus Wattles, a Quaker educator from Goshen, Connecticut, came to the conclusion that there were some four thousand African Americans in Cincinnati who were "totally ignorant of everything calculated to make good citizens."[264] He attributed their plight to the fact that many of them had been slaves and were denied the customary avenues for moral improvement.

In 1835, while attending the Anti-Slavery Convention at Putnam (now part of Zanesville), Wattles read a report on their condition: "There is still a large number who are working out their own freedom, their papers are retained as security. One man has just given his master seven notes of $100 each on which he intends to pay every year. After paying for himself he intends to buy his wife and then the children."[265]

Wattles suggested that only about 1,200 of the blacks in Cincinnati were actually free. The rest were in the process of buying their freedom, much like indentured servants. "I had travelled into almost every neighborhood of colored people in the State," he later wrote, "and laid before them the benefits of a permanent home for themselves and of the education of their children. In my first journey through the State I established, by the assistance and co-operation of Abolitionists, twenty-five schools for colored children."[266]

With respect to those in Cincinnati, Wattles proposed that they purchase land in the countryside so they would no longer be exposed to "those contaminating influences which had so long crushed them in our cities and villages."[267] A number of black families were willing to do so and commit to being farmers, provided that he would go with them and teach school. He subsequently traveled to various sites in Indiana, Michigan and even Canada but finally settled on a large plot of land in Mercer County, primarily in Butler, Marion, Granville and Franklin Townships. Along with fifteen black families, he relocated from Cincinnati toward the end of August 1835, making the trip by oxcart.

Upon their arrival in Mercer County at the beginning of October, the settlers worked cooperatively to fell trees, make clapboards and shingles and erect cabins in preparation for winter. They also cleared the land for the spring planting, while the women gathered various roots and herbs for medicinal purposes. In a letter published in the *Philanthropist* on July 19, 1840, Wattles was optimistic about the community's agricultural prospects:

> *Our settlement is progressing finely. We expect at least 250 additional men settlers this year….My doubts are all over about barbers and others who have never been farmers, being able to make their living on the land. We have two here who get along the best of any. Some of them have boarders, who attend our school, and in a year or two we shall be able to accommodate all that come. Our school varies from 16 to 30 as they can be spared from the work on the farm. There are over fifty who attend at different times.*[268]

However, he had raised only $300 of the $2,000 he needed to erect a schoolhouse and other buildings on his property. He had hoped that the Friends of the American Anti-Slavery Society would help finance his vision.

In a letter addressed to the *Xenia Free Press* dated November 1, 1840, a correspondent who professed to be acquainted with every family in the community wrote:

Among those settled here are some of the most wealthy and respectable from our populous cities. Others who have purchased their freedom at exorbitant prices have only been able since to lay up $50 to $100 to purchase their forty or eighty acres of land on which they now lived. Here they have settled down in comfortable homes, under their own vine and fig-tree, with none to molest or make them afraid.[269]

When Celina, the county seat of Mercer County, was preparing to contruct its first brick buildings, a man named W. Riley was looking to hire workers to mould and burn the brick they would need. However, he found no takers among the white men in the vicinity. He appealed to Wattles for help, and a number of the African American settlers jumped at the opportunity to earn money as brickmakers. However, as Riley later wrote: "At this juncture the very white men who had refused to do the work made pretense of being anxious and determined to drive the negroes off by warning them out of town as paupers."[270] But because they had jobs and Riley had rented them log cabins in Montezuma, Franklin Township, there was nothing the white men could do about it.

On December 28, 1840, a "mulatto" settler named Charles Moore platted the village of Carthagena in sixty-four lots.[271] Four Protestant churches, including a Baptist and a Methodist, the earliest in 1841, and three schools were built here. All of the churches were razed during the 1930s, and the schools were integrated, consolidated and eventually closed. Charles was the third son of Dorcas Moore. According to county records, she and her eight children had been emancipated by "Mrs. Elizabeth Moore, on August 25, 1826, of the county of Harrison, Kentucky, now a resident in Clermont County."[272]

Historian Anna-Lisa Cox observed that African Americans living in Cleveland received letters from the black farmers in Carthagena, inviting them to relocate. They asked them if they "would not be serving your country and your race to more purpose, if you were to leave your present residences and employments and go into the country and become a part of the bone and sinew of the land?"[273]

Over the years, Wattles and roughly six hundred black families purchased nearly 10,000 acres of land. The wealthiest of the settlers, a man named Smoyer, purchased 520 acres, all in Granville Township. Of the total, Wattles purchased 190 acres of his own in 1837 and established a school of manual labor catering to African American boys. He operated the school at his own expense until November 11, 1842, at which time the property was purchased by the trustees of the late Samuel Emlen Jr., a Quaker from New Jersey.[274]

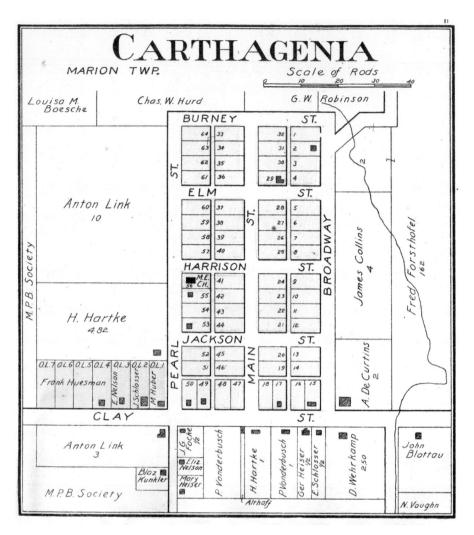

Charles Moore is credited with platting the village of Carthagena (not "Carthegenia").
Authors' collection.

The previous winter, Wattles had met with the trustees and learned that Emlen had left $20,000 in his will for the "support and education in school learning and the mechanical arts and agriculture, boys, of African and Indian descent, whose parents would give them up to the school."[275] Following the purchase, Wattles was appointed superintendent of the newly named Emlen Institute. It was modeled after the Manual Labor School of Emanuel von Fellenberg of Hofwyl, Switzerland. Word of the school soon reached the South, and many African Americans began arriving.

Augustus Wattles founded the Emlen Institute as a trade school for all. *Authors' collection.*

With a vocal minority on record as opposing the presence of African American settlers in Mercer County, Wattles felt increasing pressure from neighboring citizens to close the institute, which was viewed as a magnet drawing them to Carthagena. Finally, in 1857, he did.[276] The community would grow no larger.[277]

Among the settlers were William H. Jones and his wife, Mary. William, the son of Samuel and Mary Jones, was from Kentucky, but was free born because his father had bought his own freedom at the age of thirty. After a year in Liberia, a colony being promoted by those who felt all slaves should return to Africa, Samuel returned to the United States and made his way to Mercer County in 1839. By 1882, William had "filled the office of supervisor, school director, and clerk."[278]

Ishmael and Agnes Keith settled in Mercer County in 1842. Five years later, their son, Robert Keith, purchased two hundred acres of land and became a farmer. He also served as a township trustee. In 1851, he married Francis Harper and had a son. Robert's "grandfather was John Marshall Keith, and a nephew of Chief Justice Marshall, who was a lawyer and planter in the State of Georgia."[279]

Wilson and Martha Handly Cowell settled in Butler Township in 1850. Their son James, who was born in West Virginia, married Mary Power of Toledo and became a farmer near Carthagena. "His maternal ancestors

[were] John and Betsy Power, who settled in Mercer County in 1850."[280] The father of three children, James was the school director for a time and also a deacon in the Baptist Church.

Born in Virginia, George W. Smith Came to Mercer County in 1854. He was already married to Elizabeth Moreland of Tennessee. Their family consisted of seven children, two of whom had died before 1882. After living near Carthagena for six years, the Smiths moved to Butler Township, where they purchased "eighty acres, which he first improved, and then purchased another forty-acre tract."[281]

Then there was Henry and Catherine Harper, who arrived in 1857, with their nine-year-old son, Harry. They had been granted their freedom in the will of John Harper of Randolph County, North Carolina. Little Harry would go on to hold the office of village constable for three years and director of the schools for another seven "In 1878, he married Anna, daughter of John and Anna Barnes, of [Mercer] county."[282]

While conducting genealogical research in Philothea, Butler Township, Allen Bernard discovered that during 1857–58, sixty-four African Americans were baptized at St. Mary Catholic Church, primarily by John Vanderbrook. In addition, an African American woman was accepted into the Himmelgarten Convent of Mary, Mother of God. This suggests that they enjoyed a good relationship with their German American neighbors.

Two biracial clergymen from Carthagena, Sam Jones and Harrison Lee, are known to have been active in the Underground Railroad. In addition, eight local men enlisted in Company B, Fifty-Fifth Massachusetts Volunteer Infantry. They were George W. Akers, George W. Bush, Fortunatus Craig, Eli Hall, Charles Mackerfield, Weston H. Moore, James H.G. Moss and Thomas R. Overton.

The Fifty-Fifth Massachusetts was the sister regiment of the Fifty-Fourth Massachusetts Volunteers. They were formed after President Abraham Lincoln enacted on the Emancipation Proclamation on January 1, 1863, opening the doors for men of color, free and ex-slave, to enlist in the Union army. The Fifty-Fifth was created to handle the overflow as African Americans from Massachusetts and other states continued to arrive.

In 1867, the *Cincinnati Commercial* published a letter by a correspondent who had spent thirteen days visiting with African Americans in both Rumley and Carthagena. He wrote:

I was told that the colored settlers were shiftless, and but barely lived by such culture as they gave their farms. I have found that the majority more

Left: George Akers joined the Fifty-Fifth Massachusetts and was made a nurse. *Jim Bowsher collection.*

Right: Carthagena resident "Fannie" Taylor's biography was published by her husband and son. *Jean Miller.*

than live by the culture of their farms, that in all years of fair crops they increase in worldly gear and the goods of life. I was prepared to find them in almost all cases blessed with sufficiency, in many cases with abundance. I was told they lived from hand to mouth. I have found many of their smoke houses rejoicing in plenty, and their farms bursting with abundance.[203]

The writer observed that he had heard men who didn't pay a dollar a year to support the schools or jails or other public institutions say that "that it would be a burning shame for niggers to vote," while he found black men paying up to $300 a year in taxes to support the same institutions, which systematically ignored them, and to pay a debt brought about by their patrons and oppressors, in other words, the enormous debt incurred as the result of the Civil War.

Sandy "Mack" McCray began writing friendly letters to "Fannie" Taylor, a resident of Carthagena, in January 1868 and presumably continued to do so until their marriage in October 1869. As he noted, "My first letter of courtship to our subject was accepted.…There had been but little courting, and that had been done by correspondence."[284] Fannie would have required the assistance of someone who could read and write to compose the letters she sent back in response to those she received from Mack. Perhaps someone like Nicey E. Bush.

While the McCrays' correspondence has not survived, three courtship letters exchanged between another couple during this period have. Nicey Bush, a black woman living in Carthagena, wrote to Harvey Moore, a black man in nearby Coldwater, in September and December 1869. Harvey was the son of Dorcas Moore and brother of Charles. Theirs were probably more traditional love letters, at least as can be judged by the three that have survived.

In the first known letter, dated September 14, 1869, Nicey pours out her feelings: "There is something that compels me to write—yet something I have tried to keep which I cannot retain any longer that is live, yes, I love you. You have stolen my heart."[285] She then begs Harvey for forgiveness for having sometimes ignored his letters and confesses that her heart would break if he treated her in that manner. She concludes with, "I don't expect you can read this if you cant [*sic*] I will read it for you."[286] This suggests that their situation was the reverse of that of Sandy and Fannie: she was the one who could read and write and he couldn't.

The former Carthagena home of J.T.A. Bostwick, a black schoolteacher and postmaster. *Author photo.*

Harvey, in his response, dated October 26, 1869, insists that he would never knowingly hurt her and that it was he who had been neglectful. "My heart had bin stolen and I believe it's you that has in its possession, would you be willing to give me yours in return or would you refuse or persist in refusing to speak on this most solemn subject, subject of matrimony."[287] He concludes, "I have something I call a condisional [sic] proposition that I wish to make to you."[288]

The final surviving letter is dated December 20, 1869. In it, Harvey begins, "Dear Nicey, I must call you by that little name." This suggests Nicey was a nickname or pet name and not her real name. He then goes on to ask her, "Well Nicey when shall that happy day bee, please decide the doubtful case, you may ask what day our wedding day, you must get your excuses ready."[289] After requesting a private meeting with Nicey, he then writes, "I don't see how you can afforde to attach your self to one so limited in point of education circumstances and every other material consideration remember that notwithstanding I have commended my self to you, willing to shear all the joys and sorrows of life with you."[290]

As of 1880, Harvey and Nicey were living in Carthagena.

Miami County

Rossville, Hanktown and Marshalltown

Rossville Settlement (Spring Creek Township)

Thirteen years after the death of their master, 383 formerly enslaved individuals arrived in Piqua, Ohio. In his last will and testament, John Randolph not only granted them their freedom but also earmarked funds to help settle them in a free state. They had just completed an arduous journey of five hundred miles from Randolph's plantation in Roanoke, Virginia, to what was to be their new home. But as they were preparing to disembark from the canalboats to walk the last few miles to the land that had been purchased for them in Mercer County, they were confronted by a mob of angry farmers who prevented them from going any farther.

Forced to retreat, the migrants "turned back to Newport, but meeting the same kind of a reception, continued on down the canal to Piqua, where they were unloaded."[291] They then set up a camp "in a bend of the Great Miami river, on the evening the 4th of July, 1846," one newspaper recounted. "It was a sad independence day to them."[292] During their prolonged encampment, the ex-slaves were an object of much curiosity. Visitors were entertained by their "plantation jigs and…unintelligible songs."[293] The young boys would dance for hours for the dimes and quarters tossed to them as they sang, "I build my house in Baltimore, Three stories high."[294]

At the end of the month, a correspondent brought readers up to date on the ongoing ordeal of the former slaves. A.H. Gerrard wrote, "After being

Jimmy "Jeems" Rial rose from slavery to affluence before ending his days in poverty. *Piqua Public Library.*

driven from Mercer county by the Dutch and Whiskey, led on by Lawyers of St. Mary's, they encamped at Piqua, and awaited the arrival of Judge Leigh."[295] Judge William Leigh, Randolph's close friend, had been selected to oversee the process of relocating the former slaves. He had originally hired an agent to carry it out but now felt a need to personally intervene.

Since there was already an African American colony in Rumley, Shelby County, thought was given to settling some of the formerly enslaved people there and also in Miami County. Some land had allegedly been purchased for that purpose. However, when Judge Leigh reached Sidney, the county seat of Shelby County, he received a message from Reverend W.B. Spencer, Judge Patrick G. Goode, James Blair, Hugh Thompson and others who objected to efforts to find a new home for the African Americans. Although Leigh said he was "unacquainted with the character" of the refugees, he decided "it would be useless to attempt to settle them in a community where the Judges and Ministers rise up in opposition."[296] Consequently, he issued orders to make preparations for their return to Virginia.

During the next two hours, however, an ad hoc group of "friends of the Randolph slaves" polled the local populace and concluded that very few of them wanted to drive the settlers away. Despite the fact that they had already boarded the canalboats, a Dr. Mason was able to prevail on Judge Leigh not to leave until after a meeting could be called to gauge the public mood. It did not prove to be necessary. By evening, Goode, Spencer and Thompson had dropped their opposition. The general opinion was that the ex-slaves could be settled on the lands purchased for them without serious difficulty. Half of them were moved to the property the next day. The remainder were transported to their new home on Monday.

The opposition then renewed its efforts to drive the black families out of the county. A mob of roughly one hundred men surrounded their Piqua encampment and angrily commanded Judge Leigh to take them and leave. Intimidated by the mob and fearing their property would be destroyed if they refused, he went back to Sidney. "A public meeting was called that night at the Court House which was full, and without a dissenting voice, passed resolutions recognizing their right to settle—rebuking the exhibition of *mob spirit*, and pledging themselves to turn out if called on *to sustain the laws and protect the negroes*."[297]

Although several of the community's best and wealthiest citizens approached Leigh the next day and offered to take charge of the group and ensure they got settled, he was reluctant to take the risk. He preferred to go back to Virginia and then take them to either Trinidad or Liberia. Nevertheless, the citizens continued to lobby the judge and he finally agreed to leave 150 of them behind. The remainder were scattered to Piqua, Troy, Sidney and elsewhere. In the end, only James Blair continued to object to their settlement.

Black children in Rossville attended their own school taught by black teachers. *Piqua Public Library.*

Fountain Randolph, one of the original settlers, later recalled, "The good citizens of Piqua allowed us to land here and use as temporary camping grounds, part of what is now E. Ash St," Fountain said. "We did not know how long we would be able to remain here and thought we might be sent back to Virginia. But a meeting was called in the city hall and it was decided that we would be allowed to stay here and that homes would be provided for us."[298]

In 1878, the *New York Sun* published an article about John Randolph's slaves that included "Facts about This Curious Colony Never Before Told."[299] Randolph purportedly owned close to one thousand slaves but never sold any and only bought one and that was because the slave's master was abusing him. However, by the time the slaves were emancipated, their numbers had been reduced to fewer than four hundred. For whatever reason, they included many elderly men and women who were "far advanced in helplessness. The proportion of able-bodied middle-aged men and women to children and old people was noticeably small."[300]

Fortunately, there were many citizens at Piqua who were eager to help them. "With the ready money he had in his possession, [Judge Leigh] bought small homesteads for the older members of the colony, in a suburb of the city, and found situations as laborers for the young men, and places as house servants for the young women—in many places securing homes for entire families on farms, and thus preventing, as far as possible, the separation of parents and children."[301] Fountain said that they remained in the camp for about a year. During that time, people would come to see them and choose the family they wanted to assist. "My mother and I were sent to the Blue farm," just east of the river, where they remained for about a year.[302] From there, they went to a farm on Staunton Street and then to a dense woods on Washington Pike, which was part of the Moody farm.

The *Cincinnati Gazette* reported that "farmers around Troy and Sidney have taken possession of the negroes, and given them quarters."[303] Other newspapers mentioned they had been "distributed among families who are teaching them to read, and training to habits of industry and frugality."[304] The *New York Sun* stated, "They had everything to learn. Plantation methods of work would not answer on Ohio farms, and men and women had to be taught, like children, to perform the most simple operations."[305] Eventually, the freedmen and women collected in three Miami County communities: Rossville, Marshalltown and Hanktown. However, the Rossville colony was the largest and most successful.

"Directly to the north and east of Piqua across the great Miami river is the village of Rossville," historian John Hyer wrote, "platted in 1840, and named after a man by the name of Ross who established a carding mill on that side of the river."[306] Because of its proximity to Piqua, Rossville had no businesses of its own, so the residents had to do their shopping for groceries and other necessities on the other side of the river. Originally a white community, it acquired a significant African American population in the years following the arrival of the former Randolph slaves in 1846. And, for the most part, they lived there unmolested. Those who had trade skills, such as York Rial, who had been a stonemason, were hired to build homes. Others took odd jobs wherever they could.

Rossville's "African" cemetery was named for Jackson Ross, a black attorney. *Author photo.*

Just over ten years later, on February 18, 1857, William Rial purchased lot no. 13 from W.W. McFarland, a white man. Here he erected his house and also laid out the African Cemetery (later renamed Jackson Cemetery) in which many of the former slaves would find their final resting places. This would become the heart of the Rossville Settlement. Civil War veterans Peer M. Bray, John Cain, Henry Clay, Johnson Crowder, William Kendall, H. Parsley, John Taylor, Sidney Vicks and Phillip White are interred there.

The first church services in Rossville were held in Polly White's house in 1857. The African Baptist Church was built in 1860. The elder members of the black community were particularly anxious that the children receive a good education, so they used part of the money that had been set aside for them to hire a teacher to manage their school. The first black school in Rossville opened in 1873.

Tellingly, the number of African American property owners had dropped from fourteen in 1850 to two in 1860. Researcher Connie Porcher noted that in 1850, "Sampson Riley, Shadrack White, Guy Howell, and Gabriel White, all listed as laborers, owned property worth a combined total of $950. This figure is all the more significant when compared to white property ownership in Rossville which totaled only $1,100."[307] However, in 1860, only Shadrack and Gabriel still owned property. The most prominent black surnames were Abbott, Clark, Coleman, Howell, Jones, Lee, Randolph, Sowell, Tucker, White and Williams.

"Goodrich Giles, whose parents were enslaved on the Roanoke Plantation, was the first Black citizen to run for Piqua City Council in 1885, and again in 1886 and 1887."[308] Although he narrowly lost each time, Goodrich partnered with Carl P. Anderson in 1927 to build the Classic Theatre in downtown Dayton. It was one of the few theaters built to serve the black community.

York Rial had been brought by his parents, Guy Rial and Martha Cox, from the Randolph plantation. Except for a few years in Dayton, he lived the rest of his life in the Piqua area, primarily in Rossville. "He was honest, hard-working and self-respecting and was highly esteemed by many white people."[309] In 1905, York Rial and Nettie Harris, both of Rossville, were married in Troy, Ohio, by the Reverend Joseph Moten. It was the second marriage for both. The year before, he and Joe Moten had initiated a suit on behalf of the surviving Randolph slaves to recover the estimated 3,200 acres of land in Mercer County that had been denied them in 1846.

In time, the suit would comprise twenty-seven cases and 170 heirs. The defendants were Bernard and Anna Maria Dewall, who had been living on the property for fifty years. Finally, after a ten-year battle, the U.S. Supreme

When the Great Miami River flooded in 1913, much of Rossville was washed away. *Authors' collection.*

The Rossville home of former Randolph slave York Rial. *Author photo.*

Court upheld the original ruling by the Mercer County Court of Common Pleas that Ohio's twenty-one-year statute of limitations precluded them from recovering the land. However, York Rial passed away in 1913 of acute uremic poisoning. Joseph Morten died later the same year of a heart attack, possibly brought on by the stress of the court case.

About a century after it was founded, Rossville pretty much vanished. The late Helen Gilmore, who was descended from William and York Rial, ran the Rossville Historic House Museum for many years out of her home, the former York Rial House. Dating to back to 1890, if not earlier, it is the last remaining building to have been constructed for a former Randolph slave.

HANKTOWN (UNION TOWNSHIP)

Eighty-nine of the Randolph slaves settled in Hanktown, not far from the village of Laura. They had been taken under the wing of the Wesleyan Methodist Church in Union Township, "whose membership was made up largely of former members of the antislavery meeting of the Society of

Friends."[310] Reverend Elijah Coate and Andrew Stephens, church trustees, purchased 118 acres of land for forty families with the surnames Brown, Cloy, Cole, Cox, Giffon, Gillard, Green, Harris, Jefferson, Johnson, Moten, Thomas, Tucker, White and Young.

For the most part, Hanktown—named after James Hanks, a local surveyor—was never more than a farming community, although some residents also took jobs as day laborers. Under the leadership of Reverend Henderson Cole, they erected a log meetinghouse—the Hanktown Baptist Church—and the Hanktown School. They also set aside land as a cemetery.

Seven sons of Hanktown would serve in the Union army during the Civil War and are buried in the cemetery: Harrison Gillard, Israel White, Silas White and Spencer White all served in the Fifty-Fifth Massachusetts Colored Infantry; Hillery White was in the Fifth United States Colored Infantry and Julius Young the Fifth United States Heavy Artillery; and James Gillard's unit cannot be determined. "Of these, Harrison Gillard, Hillery White who was killed in action, Silas White and Julius Young were buried near Ludlow Creek along the northern part of the Hanktown tract."[311] Five other men from Hanktown also served in the military but are buried elsewhere: Beverly Harris, Nicholas Johnson, Peter Jones, Joseph Moten and Benjamin Williams.

Ohio contributed more volunteers to the Fifty-Fifth Massachusetts Colored Infantry than any other state. *Authors' collection.*

All that remains of the Hanktown Cemetery, including the headstones of four soldiers. *Author photo.*

Genealogist Connie Porcher discovered that "the 1850 census counts 90 blacks living in the township itself with two other young children living with white families in West Milton. While most of the men are listed as laborers, the group did claim a combined estate valued at $1,540."[312] Ten years later, "the 93 Randolph Slaves were still living as a group within the township. One member, Isaac Cole, age 67, is listed as a farmer who owned land valued at $2,000 and had a cash estate of $370."[313]

Joseph Moten, who had also been born in Roanoke and lived in Hanktown, died in 1913. A friend of York Rial, he had served in Company A, Twenty-Seventh Regiment, Ohio Colored Infantry, during the Civil War. He was married to Roseanna "Rosa" White.

Historian Gale Honeyman recalled a story she heard from Jim Hall. While laying railroad tracks near Hanktown in 1882, Hall was approached by one of the residents, who asked if he could have a railroad tie. Jim said the man "was told that if he could lift it by himself, it was his."[314] Much to their amazement, he picked it up and proceeded to carry it home.

As was true of most of the black settlements, Hanktown offered few opportunities to subsequent generations, and they began to leave. By 1900, most had departed for the cities. The last resident to be buried in the Hanktown Cemetery was Ky Jefferson, who lived with several different white families over the years, working for his room and board, until he passed away in 1931.

MARSHALLTOWN (NEWTON TOWNSHIP)

On October 16, 1847, Simon Gillard, Stephen Gillard, Lott Hill and William Young purchased several tracts of land from John and Sarah Marshall. The Marshalls were a pioneering family in Newton Township. John Marshall was the eldest son of William Marshall and had made the seven-hundred-mile journey from South Carolina in a wagon with his parents.

The Gillards, Hills and Youngs were all former Randolph slaves, and they were about to establish a community of freed African Americans in the extreme western part of Miami County near Pleasant Hill. Many of their neighbors were members of the Society of Friends, who were generally tolerant of people of color settling among them. Other surnames were Jefferson, Riggen, Taylor, White and Wright.

Marshalltown was an agrarian community throughout its one-hundred-year existence. Fittingly, all that remains is an empty field.

MUSKINGUM COUNTY

The Lett Settlement

THE LETT SETTLEMENT (MEIGS TOWNSHIP)

The story of the Lett family is the story of America, perhaps even more so now than when it was unfolding. In 1683, Molly Welsh, an English dairymaid, arrived in the Province of Maryland. Molly was white, possibly blonde, with a light complexion. She had been accused of theft—falsely, it was said—but her life was spared because she could read. So, instead, she was sent to the colonies as an indentured servant to a tobacco farmer.

Seven years later, having worked off her indenture, Molly was able to purchase a modest farm for herself. As her farm began to prosper, she reached the point where she required help to work it. According to a family history, "Although Molly was opposed to slavery, her survival left her with very few options."[315] So she bought two slaves to assist her. Later on, after she freed them, she took one as her husband. His name was Bannaka. Described as "a man of bright intelligence, fine temper, with a very agreeable presence, dignified manners and contemplative habits," he purportedly was an African prince from Senegal before being enslaved.[316]

Needing a suitable surname for the family, Molly took Banneky. Mr. and Mrs. Banneky had four daughters, the oldest named Mary. Like her mother, she married a former slave as well. His name was Robert, and he also took the Banneky surname, which morphed into Banneker. A native of Guinea, Robert had been sold into slavery but escaped and was recaptured on several occasions. Eventually, he was purchased by a master who felt that Robert carried himself with such dignity that it was not proper for him to be held in bondage any longer so he was granted his freedom.

Mary and Robert Banneker were the parents of one son—Benjamin—and four daughters. A largely self-taught mathematician and astronomer, Benjamin is recognized as the first African American man of science. He is credited with building one of the first functioning wooden clocks in the American colonies, as well as the publication of five almanacs that capitalized on his knowledge of astronomy.

Jemima Banneker, Benjamin's sister, married Samuel Lett of Baltimore County, Maryland, in 1757. A farmer of mixed English, Irish and Native American ancestry, Samuel was the son of a white woman named Delaney who later married Zachariah Lett, who was biracial. Thereafter, he adopted his father's surname. Samuel and Jemima Lett had nine children, eight of whom reached adulthood. They included Aquilla, Meshack, Elijah, Mary "Mollie," Keziah "Kizzie," Peter and Benjamin.

There is some debate regarding the first people of color to arrive in what became known as the Lett Settlement. According to Lett descendant Turner Simpson Jr., Meshack and Aquilla Lett moved to Ohio from Maryland in 1825 (some accounts say as early as 1819). They first went to Belmont County. However, Meshack, the older of the two, was not satisfied with their prospects and continued on to Meigs Township, Muskingum County. The others soon followed. The Letts were, Simpson noted, of German ancestry. The following year, Turner Simpson Sr. and Benjamin Caliman arrived. Simpson "took up the last piece of land homesteaded by a colored man in the Lett Settlement, that being the forty-acre tract directly across the road from Coal Hill Post Office."[317]

However, Robert Lett's research suggests that Moses Caliman, a white man, and his mixed-race family came earlier. After moving from New Jersey to Maryland, he married Henrietta Pearl, who was likely biracial. By 1820, the couple had migrated to Ohio with their three children, listed as indentured servants. He eventually owned nine hundred acres of land in Muskingum County. The Calimans had the following children: Mary "Polly" (who married Benjamin Lett), Elizabeth (who married Elijah Lett), Margaret (who married Lloyd E. Guy), Phoebe W. (who married Isaac Stevenson), Ann (who married Amos Guy) and Benjamin (who married Elizabeth Pearl or Perrill).

Whatever the order, the Letts, Calimans and Simpsons were quickly followed by Browns, Cliffords, Earleys, Guys, Tates, Pointers and others—

generally families with whom they were joined by ties of kinship. The Lett Settlement was composed of various tracts of land purchased during the 1820s in Meigs Township, Muskingum County, before expanding into adjoining townships in adjacent counties. Some of the settlers came there directly, but others followed more circuitous routes. For the most part, they were a self-sustaining community.

The rainbow nature of the Lett Settlement is illustrated by the rise and fall of the Wesley Chapel. As related by historian J.F. Everhart, "In the year A.D. 1824, Rev. Mordecai Bishop preached in the southeast corner of the township, and formed a class at Lazarus Marshall's."[318] Hosted by Lazarus Marshall and his wife, Mary, the fledgling Bible study class was composed of both blacks and whites.

The group continued to meet on a regular basis in private homes until 1836, when they built a log church and named it Wesley Chapel. However, as the church continued to grow, "vile self got in."[319] Some of the members began to have qualms about worshipping in the same building with people of a different race, especially when it came to taking communion at the same table. The situation became so tense that in 1843 twenty-three of the "colored members" withdrew.[320] They then built a log church in which they conducted their own services for the next eleven years until it mysteriously burned down. Three years later, they built a new structure, which they called Pleasant Hill Church. As for Wesley Chapel, it continued to lose members until it finally closed.

The locus of activity for the Lett Settlement was the now vanished village of Zeno. For a time, there was a post office and a country store, but never much else, although it did support a community orchestra during the late 1800s. However, it was briefly the residence of J.R. Clifford, who became West Virginia's first African American attorney,

Before leaving Maryland, Aquilla Lett married Christina "Charity" Cobbler. They had at least ten children. Meshack, Aquilla's brother, was married four times. His first wife was Rosannah "Roddie" Cummings, "a half-breed Indian," followed by Amelinza Wallace, Susan Stewart Lett and Mary "Mollie" Goings. Mary was the daughter of Jason Goings and Hannah Findlay. Her brothers, George and Joel Goings (or Goins), were the founders of a free black settlement in Shelby County, Ohio, called Rumley. Following Meshack's death, Mary married Benjamin Simpson.

The Lett settlers were also civil rights pioneers who challenged the State of Ohio for such things as the right to vote and access to education. They argued—sometimes successfully, sometimes not—that as taxpayers they were entitled to the same benefits as the state's white residents. The most famous incident occurred in 1845. Aquilla Lett, described as a "quadroon" who owned a farm and paid his taxes, wanted nothing more than to provide his children with an education. However, taxes were used to fund only white schools.

With that in mind, Aquilla sent his daughter Margaret, age twelve, and two younger children, Henry and Susan, to the school that served his district. (Other accounts say he sent his three daughters—"nearly women grown").[321] "The news soon spread like wild-fire that there were 'niggers in the school.'" When the school's directors heard what occurred, they ordered the student's teacher, Miss Louisa Harmon from McConnelsville, to put them in a corner by themselves until they could convene a meeting. However, Margaret refused, arguing that she "was not a nigger."[322]

On the following day, the directors once more ordered Miss Harmon to separate the students. This time, she refused to comply, asserting that they were attentive and well behaved and she would not single them out in such a humiliating manner. Furthermore, she declined to point them out to the directors. David McCarty, one of the directors, then asked Margaret, "Say, my gal, ain't you one of them?"[323] When she asked him one of what, he replied, "Why, Africans." Margaret responded that she was as white as he was. (She purportedly had a light complexion and straight, sandy-colored hair.)

At this point, Jacob Wharton, another director, tried to pick the three children out, only to find he had chosen McCarty's daughter by mistake. Predictably, when McCarty took a stab at it, he chose Wharton's daughter. Not knowing what else to do, the three men fired the obstinate teacher.

After his property was threatened with destruction, Aquilla finally decided to seek protection in the law. He filed suit against the school directors in December 1846 and won. As a result, a separate schoolhouse was built on land owned by J. Lett, and a separate fund was created for the education of children of color.

During the Columbus Convention of Colored Citizens of Ohio in 1849, a group of black women threatened to stage a boycott unless they were allowed to participate on an equal basis with the black men. Their leader was Mary Jane Pointer Merritt. Born in Pennsylvania just eighteen years earlier, she had grown up in Lett Settlement with her parents, Thomas Pointe Sr. and Nancy Butler Pointer. Her family was involved in the local Underground Railroad.

Mary and her husband, Thomas Jefferson Merritt, attended the convention in Columbus, where she presented the resolution demanding an equal voice. It read, in part, "Whereas we the ladies have been invited to attend the Convention, and have been deprived of voice, which we the ladies deem wrong and shameful. Therefore, Resolved, That we will attend no more after tonight, unless the privilege is granted."[324] Though two delegates were opposed, the resolution was passed. History had been made, if only in a small way.

By 1850, the Lett family was concentrated in the Lett Settlement in Muskingum and Guernsey Counties, as well as Payne's Crossing in Hocking and Perry Counties, Rumley in Shelby County and Stillguest/Hick's Settlement in Ross County.

Charles Lucas, a resident of Meigs Township and husband of Rachel Lett, voted in the 1853 election after the courts had ruled that a man could do so as long as he had more white than black blood in his veins. Since he had voted for the incumbent party, his vote was not further challenged. Then in 1864, Joseph Tate and several other "colored" men sought to vote but were denied by a majority of the trustees. As a result, Tate sued them, but the case did not come to trial before the election had passed. When Tate and several others attempted to vote in the next election, they were rebuffed again. This time, Aquilla Lett and four others filed suit against the trustees for denying them their right to vote. In February 1865, he won a judgment of $240 in damages against two of the trustees and the township paid it. A second suit was also won, but this time the trustees had to bear the costs themselves.

A Muskingum County history related, "The Lett Settlement produced Underground Railroad operatives Joshua Simpson and Tom and Maria Pointer, abolitionist writers Lloyd Guy and David Lett, attorneys J.R. Clifford and James H. Guy, and many others."[325] It was regarded as a safe haven in the antebellum period. However, about 1860, members of the Lett Settlement began to move away. A significant number of them settled in Michigan, specifically Mecosta County. The first African American to purchase land there was James Guy, whose first wife was Ann Mariah Caliman. When she died, he married Francis Norman. In the years that followed, many other members of the Lett community—Letts, Calimans and Tates—moved north to join them.

In December 1867, the *Zanesville Courier* was complimentary in its description of a large black settlement located nearby in Meigs Township. It said that the residents were "thrifty, industrious, inoffensive, many of them excellent farmers, and several of them quite wealthy, and own considerable tracts of land."[326]

The Lett Settlement families still continue to hold annual reunions at various places in Ohio. The most prominent surnames during its history were Brown, Caliman, Clifford, Earley, Green, Guy (or Gay), Harper, Lett (or Leth), Lucas, Pinter, Simpson and Tate (or Teate).

PAULDING COUNTY

Middle Creek or Upthegrove Settlement

MIDDLE CREEK OR UPTHEGROVE SETTLEMENT (WASHINGTON TOWNSHIP)

In his "Traveling Notes" for December 8, 1886, historian Henry Howe recorded his impressions of Paulding County: "This is about the wildest county in Ohio. It is a new county, but rapidly improving….The town is emerging from the forest and has a very primitive, woodsy look."[327]

Formed in 1839, Paulding County was originally set aside for use by Ohio's Indian tribes in the Treaty of Greenville. It was not particularly amenable to settlement because nearly all of it was located in the Great Black Swamp, a vast glacial wetlands measuring 40 miles wide and 120 miles long. Virtually impassable, it was a notorious breeding ground for "ague" (malaria). As a result, only a few hardy souls chose to live there.

Architectural historian Mary Ann Brown wrote about the Middle Creek Settlement, which "lay on the west side of the Miami-Erie Canal in the southeast corner of Paulding County. It was situated along the Auglaize Trail, used by Colonel Henry Bird as early as 1780 when he marched from Cincinnati to Detroit."[328]

Precisely when the first African Americans began arriving in Paulding County is unknown, but there likely were several waves. In 1817, Martha Upthegrove of South Carolina petitioned her husband, Henry, for "reasonable maintenance."[329] She charged that after three years of marriage,

This home near Middle Creek may have been built by black settlers. *Author photo.*

Henry began to treat her in a cruel and inhumane manner. Finally, he abandoned her to take up residence with one of his female slaves and their children. Martha asserted that Henry derived a "competent livelyhood [*sic*]" from "some land and Six or Eight negro Slaves out of [which] her the least pittance of support."[330] Her fear was that he would take his slaves and other movable property and flee the state in order to avoid paying for her support.

Martha's fears were not unfounded. In June 1840, the *Cincinnati Philanthropist* reported that "Mr. Upthegrove, of South Carolina passed through this city a few days since on his way to Clinton Co., (whither we recommended him to go) with eleven colored persons whom he had just emancipated."[331] Described as an old and rather poor man—"much attached to his people"—Upthegrove purportedly was setting them free to keep them from "falling into bad hands."[332] Some of them retained their former master's surname and may have been his children. Some of them are known to have settled in Clermont and Paulding Counties as well.

One of the manumitted slaves was John Upthegrove. Born a slave in South Carolina in 1825, he had purportedly been set free in Clinton County, Ohio, in 1835 (according to a short biography written after his death), but this does not fit the known timeline. After he grew to manhood, John moved to nearby

Fayette County, where he remained until after the Civil War in 1865. At that point, "he settled in Jackson township [Paulding County], and purchased 180 acres of land, located in Emerald and Jackson townships. He cleared this land and made improvements upon it, and it is now the residence of his widow and children."[333] John passed away in 1890, having married Phoebe J. Jones of Clinton County in 1853.

The second Upthegrove who settled in Emerald Township was Josiah. Supposedly born in Highland County, Ohio, in 1848, he was the son of Andrew Upthegrove and Susanna Rollins, "freedmen of Virginia and Carolina." His mother died when he was eighteen months old, so he was placed in the care of an uncle, Randal Upthegrove, with whom he lived until he turned eighteen. "After working a short time, he, in company with his uncle John, came to Emerald township."[334] In 1865, Josiah traveled to Greene County, where he married Carrie E. Kirk, the daughter of a former slave woman. Together, they raised six children before she died in 1885 of consumption. The owner of a 120-acre farm, Josiah was a noted breeder of horses.

At the age of two, Mary Belle Booker left "Wilford" (likely Woodford), Kentucky, with her father, William; mother, Sydney (or Sidney) Jane; and older brother, George William. Although she was too young to remember, she had been born into slavery. When their master died without heir, he left his estate to his faithful slaves. However, there was much disagreement among them about how to divide up the assets. Finally, a group of twenty-six, including the Booker family and other relations, decided to take whatever property they could and move to Ohio. In 1852, they made their way north to Paulding County and settled along Middle Creek in Washington Township.

By that time of the 1860 census, Sydney Booker was residing in the same Middle Creek household with another Kentucky family, the Bibbs. It consisted of patriarch Thomas Bibb and his three children. Genealogist Gilbert Gusler wrote, "According to Simon A. Gusler, a man named 'Bibb' freed his slaves and settled them in Washington Township on land he bought for that purpose. He came each year to look after them and brought them provisions to help them along until they learned to be self-supporting."[335]

Elias A. Dempsy was born in North Carolina, the son of two freed slaves, James Dempsy and Keturah Ashe. In 1844, at the age of five, he traveled to Clarke County, Ohio, with his parents. However, they did not remain there long. After moving to Logan County, they finally settled in Paulding County in 1863, taking up residence in Washington Township. Growing up on a farm, Elias was educated in the public schools and embarked on a career as a teacher and farmer. Married twice, Elias "held the office of township clerk for nine years and that of notary public for the same length of time," while engaged in the business of raising fine horses on his sixty-acre farm.[336]

In 1874, Mary Belle married Willis H. Dempsey, the brother of Elias, and the couple made their home in the village of Roselms. Born in Logan County in 1840, he served as pastor of the "Baptist colored church of Washington township."[337] While they had no children of their own, they raised Harry White, Etta Booker and William Dempsey.

When Mary Belle was interviewed between 1936 and 1938, she was the oldest African American residing in Paulding County. It was reported at

Elias Dempsey was a teacher, township clerk, justice of the peace, and farmer. *Laurence R. Hipp.*

the time that "most of the Negro population in Paulding County resides in Washington Township around Roselms. The chief occupation of these negroes is farming....In most cases these Negroes live in poor, dilapidated homes; the ones in Paulding have poor homes, but in the most part are much more livable than those near Roselms."[338]

Alicestyne Turley also wrote that "Baptist minister Andrew Jackson Young was born a slave in Kentucky in 1812, and eventually escaped to establish a settlement of freed blacks in Washington Township, Paulding County in 1860. He later founded the Elm Grove Baptist Church in Washington Township in 1881."[339] The 1860 census does show a family by the name of Young from Kentucky, including two Jacksons, Diannah, George, Stephen, William, Emily and Sephrona, the last born in Ohio. However, it does not list an Andrew, suggesting that the minister went by his middle name.

Charles Williams remembered the stories his father, John, used to tell him about how he came to Ohio. John said he and Charles's grandfather had fled from the Hughes Plantation somewhere in Kentucky. It is likely he was referring to a plantation by that name in Jefferson County, Kentucky, seven miles south of Louisville.

The Middle Creek Zion Baptist Church and cemetery. *Author photo.*

> *Coming from the Hughes Plantation our names would have been Hughes instead of Williams, but when granddad arrived in Ohio by way of the Underground Railroad, he changed his name to Williams to keep from being detected. My granddad bough a small acreage of land in Washington Township, Paulding County and built a small cabin on it, and began farming with his wife, Susan, my grandmother.*[340]

Major John Hughes was "the largest slave owner in Kentucky at the time of his death" in 1842.[341] While the authors of a Hughes family history were "informed, both by members of the family and by a person who visited the old plantation, that his servants were kindly cared for and very cheerful and happy," it wasn't enough to keep at least two slaves at home.[342]

When he arrived in Ohio via the Underground Railroad, John Williams changed his surname from Hughes to Williams. "My granddad," anthropologist Jill Rowe learned from one of his descendants, "bought a small acreage of land in Washington Township, Paulding County and built a small cabin on it, and began farming with his wife Susan, my grandmother."[343]

While still a teenager, Charles Williams met a young lady named Louella Goings, one of eight children reared by Doc Goings. In 1876, Doc had moved his family from Mercer County near Anna Station to Paulding

Dr. D.C. Goings was born in Rumley and later moved to Middle Creek. *Laurence R. Hipp.*

County. Although they lived nine miles apart, Charles started courting Louella on Sunday afternoons, walking the entire distance. They married about 1885 and had a dozen children who intermarried with members of the Underwood, Upthegrove, Bond, Rowe, Woods, Mines, Galloway, Ferguson, Spencer and Tipton families.

In 1892, the Paulding County atlas devoted fewer than one hundred words to the Middle Creek Settlement:

> *The township contains a colony of colored people who, for the most part, are in a thrifty and prosperous condition. Some of them are well educated and have held township offices. There are also some colored people located in Emerald, Jackson, Paulding and Blue creek townships; but the greatest number are to be found in Washington township. Many of these were formerly slaves in Kentucky, and were liberated before the war; others were born free in the southern part of the state.*[344]

Pike County

Carr's Run and Pee Pee Settlement

Carr's Run and Straight Creek Settlement (Jackson Township)

It has been well established that Waverly was a "sundown town" in which people of color knew better than to hang around after dark. Supposedly, a covenant had been written into the deed for the Pike County courthouse property stating that it would revert to the original owner "if an African American was ever allowed to settle within the town."[345]

James Emmitt, Scioto Valley's self-proclaimed first millionaire, lobbied to move the county seat from Piketon. But why would he include such a provision in the deed (assuming he did)? There is a bit of folklore to account for it. A former resident said that his uncle told him Emmitt's daughter had been impregnated by a black man. She was then disowned by her family and her lover was subsequently hanged beside the courthouse. However, there is no record of this, and no evidence has turned up supporting other aspects of the tale.

A half dozen or so African American families arrived in Pike County from Virginia about a year after Waverly was platted in 1829, settling about four miles northwest of town. Although they were said to have worked hard and did not bother anyone, some of their white neighbors resented their presence. Sometimes they even took action against them. "When Waverly was still in its swaddling clothes," historian Henry Howe wrote, *there was a "yellow nigger" named Love, living on the outskirts of the town. He was a low-minded, impudent, vicious fellow, with the cheek of a mule. He was very insulting, and made enemies on every hand. His conduct finally became so objectionable, that a lot of the better class of citizens got together one night, made a descent upon his cabin, drove him out, and stoned him a long way in his flight toward Sharonville. He never dared to come back.*[346]

Perhaps. But in 1875, a local census revealed that, although the town had 1,279 residents, "the fact of Waverly's not having a single colored resident is a rare mark of distinction for a town of its size. And what makes the fact more remarkable, there never has been a Negro or mulatto resident of the place."[347] Obviously, there was more at work than the alleged bad behavior of one man to account for "this antipathy to the Negro."[348]

An article written by Paul Schrader suggested that those African Americans who settled in Jackson Township arrived in 1823 and may have come from Monroe County, (West) Virginia. There were seventy-five of them altogether, formerly enslaved persons led by a man named Walker who was a schoolteacher and Baptist minister. "Most of the people who settled in this area," according to Schrader, "were descendants from the Walkers or Raglands."[349] However, the Raglands were not freed until 1855. They chose Jackson Township because the land was cheaper than in Ross County.

The band of migrants who accompanied Walker were exceptionally poor and had walked the entire way. All they owned was what they were able to carry. In order to survive, they had to work together and help one another build shelter, clear the land and begin raising crops. They also started a school—Walker taught from the few books he had brought with him—and a church.

Efforts to identify the enigmatic "Walker" have not been successful. There was an African American man named Thomas Walker who was born in Virginia in 1796, but it is not known when he arrived in Jackson Township. While he and his family do not appear until the 1860 census, he had at least one child who was born in Ohio as early as 1835.

John Dippel has noted that "from an agricultural perspective, Ohio was not well suited for the slave system, so even large landowners—the group that profited most from the chattel system in the South—did not advocate its introduction."[350] The migration of free blacks from Kentucky to Ohio "was a largely unforeseen and unexpected development"—not to mention racially threatening.[351] Many free or fugitive blacks from Kentucky were prompted to move just across the river to Ohio. "For them, it was the nearest and most unambiguously 'free' part of the Old Northwest, as the legal status of slavery in Indiana and Illinois was still unresolved."[352]

One of the most prominent members of the African American community in Jackson Township was Christopher Brown. His father, Elias Brown, was biracial, with a black father and a white mother. Christopher's mother, Honor Mundel, was the daughter of Robert Mundel and a woman named Judy. They were slaves of James and Betty Dawson of Maryland. Because they had no children of their own, the Dawsons "made pets of their slaves, who, consequently, led a very easy life."[353]

As James Dawson grew older, his nieces and nephews developed designs on his slaves, scheming among themselves as to how they would divide them up. When he learned of this, he declared none of them would have them. So when Honor was thirteen years old, Dawson freed all of his slaves. For some unknown reason, Robert chose to add Mundel—the surname of a former master—to his name.

In 1800, Elias Brown married Honor Mundel. The ceremony was performed at the Dawson plantation. A year later, James was born, followed by John, Enoch, Christopher, David, Elias, Elizabeth, Charles and Madison, the last in 1821. Elias, Honor and five children left Maryland in 1813, intending to go to "the Scioto bottoms where the Fosters, Lucases, Bowmans, Vanmeters, Dawsons, Moores, and other Maryland and Virginia families, their friends and acquaintances, had come on before."[354]

Upon reaching Pennsylvania, with winter approaching, the Browns decided to stay put. They settled down for eight years. Finally, in 1820, Elias left Pennsylvania with his son Christopher and came to Ohio. Christopher was left with his grandfather Robert Mundel, who had settled on Big Run, in Jackson Township, Pike County, while Elias returned to Pennsylvania for the other members of the family. They returned the following June. The Browns settled on Congress land near Pigeon Roost in adjoining Jackson County.

Robert Mundel had come to Ohio earlier than Elias to work for Joseph Foster. Four of the five Foster brothers had "settled on the rich bottoms of the Scioto river in Ross and Pike counties," while the fifth moved onto Illinois.[355] They had come from (West) Virginia. Robert held John Foster, in particular, in high regard. "They were true friends to the colored people."[356] The year after his son's death from consumption in 1827, Robert arranged for his grandson Christopher to work for Joseph Foster "during the crop raising season."[357]

"From 1828 to 1838 Christopher Brown followed farming and the rivers—principally the latter."[358] However, he found working on the river to be wretched, so in 1837 he purchased 40 acres of Congress land in Jackson Township and leased another 25 acres from John Pancake. After clearing the bottomland, he built a cabin and married Nancy Jane Lucas. In 1840, under the influence of the Reverend Thomas Woodson, Christopher Brown joined the African Methodist Episcopal Church. Three years afterward, he became a licensed preacher and was heavily involved in the Underground Railroad, conveying runaways to Chillicothe. In 1855, he sold his farm to Pancake and purchased 113 acres on Straight Creek. Christopher and Nancy had thirteen children, nine of whom survived to adulthood.

Seven fugitive slaves arrived in Jackson Township from Virginia in 1841. Agents of the Underground Railroad hid them away in the forests and caves of Jackson and Pike Counties for several days. However, two slave hunters with a pack of dogs combed the valleys and hills in pursuit of them. "As they came through Jackson county, they caught and whipped Rev. John Woodson, to compel him to tell where the fugitives were secreted. But he did not know, nor would he have told had he known."[359]

When the runaways entered Pike County, Christopher Brown was alerted. Although the slave hunters stood guard over his canoe all one night to ensure he did not offer the men any assistance, on another night he was able to smuggle them across the Scioto River and send them along toward Canada. "Four of the seven were caught supposed to have been betrayed by a man of their own color. The other two also escaped."[360]

George W. Crocker was another leader of the community. Born in Southampton County, Virginia, George was the son of Harrison Crocker. Although he lived in a slave state, he was never enslaved. "In 1846 he came to Pike County, Ohio, where slavery was unknown, and in 1860 he purchased his present farm of 225 acres, in Jackson Township."[361] He married Susan Artis in 1853, and they had one daughter. When Susan died in 1882, he married Mary Lewis. Crocker's neighbors at Carr's Run were Carter Harris, Jeremiah Harris and Augusta Zimmerman (who would also reside in Pee Pee Settlement).

A vestige of Waverly's legacy of segregation, however, is the community of East Jackson (or "E.J.") in Jackson Township. A suburb of Waverly, East Jackson remains a neighborhood "where many residents have cream-colored skin, red hair, light-colored eyes—and proudly identify as black in spite of ongoing racial attacks and the presence of white supremacist groups."[362]

Once a station on the Underground Railroad, East Jackson, also known as Carr's Run, occupied the east end of Jackson Township, while the west end was populated by white people.

Although many of the residents of East Jackson could pass for white, they self-identify as African American or person of color. They also "are enrolled in the Saponi-Catawba Nation and Catawba of Carr's Run, with documented Saponi-Catawba families such as Harris, Byrd, Scott, and Chavis."[363] This reflects kinship ties with Native Americans who lived in Ohio from before it became a state.

PEE PEE SETTLEMENT (PEBBLE TOWNSHIP)

A group of African Americans established Eden Baptist Church in 1824 on land donated by Minor Muntz in Pebble Township. Prior to that, they had been holding services in their homes. There may have been thirteen original families, and they were soon joined by others as the settlement spilled over into Huntington Township in adjoining Ross County. Because it was located on Pee Pee Creek, it became known as Pee Pee Settlement. Peter Patrick, an early squatter from Virginia, carved his initials—"P.P."—in a tree. Although Patrick and his friends were driven out of the area by the Indians, his initials remained and gave name to the creek.

Some accounts say the settlers were excellent farmers, but others claim the quality of the land was poor. Although the black settlers purportedly worked hard and did not bother anyone, some of their white neighbors resented their presence. Timothy Downing was said to be "the leader of the gang that made almost constant war" on the African Americans who had settled there.[364] "They burned their wheat and hay, harassed their livestock, and did what they could to interfere in every aspect of their lives."[365] Finally, in about 1835, Downing and his henchmen, including William Burke, raided the settlement with the intent of killing them all. However, one of the African Americans killed Downing's brother instead. Afterward, Timothy Downing went to the man's house and shot him in the head. The man survived and moved away, while Downing escaped charges.

After William Garland, a fugitive slave, found his way to Pebble Township, he joined Union Baptist Church and assisted several other members who were involved in the Underground Railroad. Mostly Virginians, "they brought a multitude of skills, talents and considerable wealth to the new community," wrote researcher Beverly J. Gray. "They built a school, meeting hall and organized a church."[366]

It would not be surprising to find that they were influenced by the Reverend David Nickens, who had organized the First Baptist Church in Chillicothe the same year. The chuch became the spiritual and social center of the community and was strongly rooted in the antislavery movement.

"Many members of the congregation were either former slaves or descendants of former slaves of President Thomas Jefferson."[367] Among them were Israel Gillette Jefferson, who had been his master's coachman, and Madison Hemings (sometimes "Hemmings"). An interview conducted with Madison Hemings by S.F. Wetmore and published in 1873 largely went unnoticed during his lifetime. However, when it was rediscovered in the early twentieth century, it provided a boost for those who argued that President Thomas Jefferson had fathered several children by his slave Sally Hemings. Derived partly from his own experience and partly from his family's oral history, Madison's story had the ring of truth.

Madison related that his grandmother was Elizabeth "Betty" Hemings, the property of John Wales, a Welshman and Martha Jefferson's father. Her mother was "a full-blooded African" (Susanna Epps) by Madison's account, while her father was a man named Hemings, captain of an English trading vessel. At the time of Mrs. Wales's passing, Elizabeth had grown to womanhood, so John Wales took her as his concubine. She bore him six children who all were given the surname Hemings.

While visiting the Wales household, Thomas Jefferson became acquainted with John's daughter, Martha. Eventually, they married, and he took his bride to live with him at Monticello. Upon the death of John Wales, Elizabeth Hemings and her six children became the property of Martha Jefferson and came to live with her at Monticello.

During this period, Jefferson's star was rising. Just as he was appointed minister to France in 1787, his wife passed, so his older daughter, Martha, accompanied him on his trip abroad. His younger daughter, Maria, was left behind. Later, she was summoned to France as well, and Sally accompanied her as a body servant. Madison related that "during that time my mother became Mr. Jefferson's concubine, and when he was called back home she was enceinte [pregnant] by him."[368] She was about fifteen years old.

Much to Jefferson's surprise, Sally refused to return home with him. "She was just beginning to understand the French language well, and in France she was free, while if she returned to Virginia she would be re-enslaved," Madison said.[369] So Jefferson promised her that if she came back with him to

Virginia, she would have "extraordinary privileges" and her children would be given their freedom when they reached the age of twenty-one.[370]

Back at Monticello, Sally bore her master six children, only four of whom survived to adulthood: Beverly, Harriett, Madison and Eston. Owing to the fact that their father and grandfather were white, Beverly (a boy) and Harriett had light complexions and could pass for white. Both married white spouses and lived as white in Washington, D.C. Eston, however, took a black wife, moved to Chillicothe, Ohio, and then on to Wisconsin in 1852.[371]

Born in 1805, Madison had detailed memories of life at Monticello and of his father, Thomas Jefferson. And, to the extent that they could be fact checked, they were true. At age fourteen, Madison was apprenticed to a carpenter, John Hemings, his grandmother's young son. In 1834, Madison married Mary McCoy, whose grandmother was a manumitted slave. At first they remained in Virginia, but in 1836, they moved to Pike County, taking up residence in Pee Pee Settlement, where he found work in his trade and raised a large family of nine children. He passed away in 1877, at the age of seventy-two.

It was Israel Jefferson's belief that he was born at Monticello, Virginia, in 1797, on Christmas Day. He was the son of a slave named Jane who was owned by Thomas Jefferson. His father was a man named Edward Gillet. About the time that Jefferson began his second term as president, Israel started working as a waiter at the family table and remained with Jefferson at Monticello until he died in 1826, when Israel was twenty-nine years old. Israel also held the position of postilion when Jefferson went out in his landau carriage, which was drawn by four horses.

Upon his death, Jefferson had arranged for seven of his slaves to be released: "Sally, his chambermaid, who took the name of Hemings, her four children—Beverly, Harriet, Madison and Eston—John Hemings, brother to Sally, and Burrell Colburn [Burwell Colbert], an old and faithful body servant."[372] All the rest were auctioned off three years later. Israel was purchased by Governor Thomas Walker Gilmer. He married a slave woman, Mary Ann Colter, and had four children before she died. "As they were born slaves," Israel related, "they took the usual course of most others in the same condition of life. I do not know where they now are, if living."[373] He then married Elizabeth Farrow Randolph, a widow, who had been free-born because her mother was white.

After Governor Gilmer was elected to Congress, he gave Israel the opportunity to purchase his freedom for $500 (the amount Gilmer had originally paid for him) plus an addition $300 "to bind the bargain."[374]

Because Elizabeth was a free woman, Israel was bought in her name. When they went to the Charlottesville Court House to obtain his emancipation certificate, the clerk suggested that Israel use Jefferson as a surname because "it would give me more dignity to be called after so eminent a man."[375] He and his wife then moved to Cincinnati. After fourteen years, they moved to Pebble Township.

In Pike County, there existed a bitter divide between those who supported slavery and those who didn't. A number of the black families and some of the whites became involved in the local Underground Railroad. Among those members who took leading roles in the UGRR were the Barnetts—James, Henry, David and their families—and their friend Minor Muntz.

Even after the Civil War, the community and the church continued to grow as African American families came north. In 1878, the church was renamed the Eden Baptist Church and a new building was erected. The Barnett Cemetery, not far from Eden Baptist Church, contains several graves of note.

Ross County

Stillguest or Hick's Settlement

Stillguest or Hicks Settlement
(Concord Township)

Thomas Worthington, father of Ohio statehood, was born near Charles Town, (West) Virginia, in 1773. Like many of the state's founding fathers, he was once a slaveholder. Along with Edward Tiffin, his brother-in-law, he decided to move from Virginia to a place near Chillicothe in what would become the state of Ohio. However, they would have to free the slaves they had inherited.

In the spring of 1798, Worthington, Eleanor Swearingen (his wife), their infant daughter and the Tiffin family made their way to Ohio. Some of their former slaves—"forty-six in number, of all ages and both sexes"—chose to accompany them.[376] On the grounds of Adena, his two-thousand-acre estate in the wilderness of Ross County, Worthington constructed cabins for the African Americans who would continue to serve him. Although Worthington had promised them "a freehold...whenever he should judge them capable of preserving the cabin and adjacent acres, which he allowed them by way of probation," none of the families would ever receive title to the land.[377]

Worthington's slaves included Amy, Mary, Henny, Richard and Caroline, per a petition filed in 1824.[378] He is also known to have owned a William Glassingale, Fanny Dearmint (or Demint), Patty Curtis (daughter of Fanny) and Judy Stanley (wife of Isaac). Of these, ninety-five-year-old Judy was

Thomas Worthington's Adena mansion once had servant cabins behind it. *Library of Congress.*

living in Union Township, in 1850, with John, Jane and Kizah Stanley, along with Samuel and Harriet Groves—all African Americans. This would have placed her close to or at the Hicks Settlement.

White Brown—"a Methodist of distinction"—was one of, if not the, earliest white settlers of Deerfield Township.[379] But he did not do it alone. "Mr. Brown was reared under the influence of slavery, and was himself the owner of forty [or sixty] slaves in his native state of Delaware. The institution became so repugnant to him that he decide to seek a home on free soil, and this led to his removal to Ohio in 1799 [or 1801]."[380] He arrived in Ross County with his sons and his slaves to begin developing five hundred acres of land, largely forest, that he had explored two years earlier.

Brown had promised his "slaves that he would give to them their freedom if they would accompany him to Ohio, assist him on his journey and in his settlement."[381] With their help, the Browns cleared the land, planted and harvested a crop of corn and built a log house. Historian J.B.F. Morgan wrote that Brown's "big heart would not allow him to keep in bondage the forty blacks he had in his possession. They were not only made free, but several of them were assisted in obtaining a livelihood."[382] It has been speculated that Tobias Hicks was one of them as well.

Along with his son, Hicks purportedly came to Ohio from Maryland at about the same time White Brown did. Somehow he was able to purchase land in Concord Township, Ross County, which became the nucleus of a settlement of African Americans that extended up into Pickaway County. It was initially known as Hicks Settlement and was located about eight miles northwest of Chillicothe.

A large number of African Americans collected there, both freedmen and woman as well as fugitive slaves who found it to be a safe haven. One of them was Joseph Stillguest (or Stillgess). He was a young runaway when Tobias adopted him. After Tobias died, Joseph continued to open his home to escaped slaves on their quest for freedom, and the community soon came to be known as Stillguest Settlement. Later, Joseph relocated to Urbana, Ohio, where he remained active in the Underground Railroad.

Perhaps the most notable resident of the Hick's Settlement, if only briefly, was John Mercer Langston. In 1844, just a few weeks before his fifteenth birthday, John was in Chillicothe when a delegation of black farmers came to see his brother, Charles H. Langston. They were seeking his help in finding a teacher for their school. "They desired to have the school open on the first Monday of November, and continue through to the first day of the following February, three full months."[383] However, Charles could not think if anyone suitable. Not knowing where else to turn, they asked Charles if he would allow them to hire John.

Upon the orders of his guardian, John had been sent to Chillicothe from Oberlin, where he was attending college, to visit his brother for a couple of weeks. The winter break was designed to allow students to take short-term teachings assignments if they so desired. However, Charles felt that John "was too young and too small to undertake to teach and manage their school."[384] The committee assured him that the students would not present any problems and would apply themselves diligently to their studies.

John was eager to take the job and promptly hired. He began teaching on the first Monday of November 1845, a month before he turned sixteen. He was the smallest person in the school save for a boy named Samuel Cox.[385] For his services, John was paid ten dollars a month in cash. He also received board, "as he consented to pass a week in each family patronizing the school, repeating his visits to the various families as necessity might require."[386]

In 1855, John would become one of the first African Americans in the nation elected to public office when he became town clerk of Brownhelm Township, Lorain County, Ohio. He also was the first dean of the law school at Howard University, first president of Virginia State University and the first black congressman from Virginia.

Historian Henry Bennett observed, "The colored race was represented among the earliest settlers of the county. Some of these were liberated slaves, whose former masters brought them to the new country as freemen, while others were born free."[387] Among the names he mentioned were Thomas Watson, Henry Evans, Nelson Piles, Samuel Nichol, Abram Nichol, Peter James and Henry Hill.

As early as 1799, Benjamin Kerns and several others—all white men—"squatted" on the High Bank prairie of Liberty Township. While not a slave owner, Kerns did employ former slaves. In 1794, David Leroy Nickens was born a slave in Virginia. When he was about ten years old, David

As a teenager, John Mercer Langston taught school at Hick's Settlement. *Library of Congress.*

and his parents obtained their freedom and moved to Ohio.

A certificate of residency was issued in the spring of 1804 for Amlick Nickens; his wife, Serah; and James, Agness, Lot, Easter, Amlick and Moses. A separate certificate was later issued for David Nickens, based on the testimony of Joseph Gardner and James Kilgore that Edward Nickens, "a coloured man," had brought him to Ross County in 1804 or 1805. Edward, a "free negro" from Virginia, conveyed David to the farm of Benjamin M. Kerrin (Kerns).[388]

David Nickens became one of the first ordained African American ministers in Ohio and helped to organize Chillicothe's First Regular African Baptist Church of Christ in 1824. The name was later changed to the First Anti-Slavery Baptist Church of Chillicothe. Over the next twelve years, David was involved in developing an educational program for black youth, working with Augustus Wattles, the progressive educator who founded a black settlement in Mercer County, and Theodore Weld, an influential abolitionist. The congregation of his church was committed to helping fugitive slaves reach freedom via the Underground Railroad.

Following the reorganization of the African Union Baptist Church—the first black church in Cincinnati—in 1835, Nickens was called to be its pastor.

David Nickens helped organize Chillicothe's First Regular African Baptist Church of Christ. *Author photo.*

"He was faithful to every trust, and earnest in manner. He accomplished much, baptized many, was loved by his people, respected by all classes, and died in the midst of his labors, deeply lamented, in 1838."[389]

The Hick's/Stillguest Settlement remained a functioning community into the early years of the twentieth century.

20

SCIOTO COUNTY

Houston Hollow

HOUSTON HOLLOW (CLAY TOWNSHIP)

On Friday, January 21, 1831, the following notice appeared in the *Portsmouth Courier*:

> *The citizens of Portsmouth are adopting measures to free the town of its colored population. We saw a paper, yesterday, with between one and two hundred names, including most of the house-holders, in which they pledged themselves not to employ any of them who have not complied with the law. The authorities have requested us to give notice that they will hereafter enforce the law indiscriminately.*[390]

Recounting this chapter in the city's history some seventy years later, historian Nelson Evans dubbed it "Black Friday." He wrote that "all the colored people in Portsmouth"—an estimated eighty individuals—"were forcibly driven out. They were forced to leave their homes and belongings." Some of them would settle in an area known as Huston Hollow, Clay Township, six miles north of town.

This was not the first time African Americans had been expelled from town. Historian Andrew Feight discovered that "at a meeting on March 2, 1818, the Wayne Township Trustees had authorized special payment of $4.18 to Warren Johnson, the town constable, for 'warning out black and mulatto persons of the township.'"[391]

Incredibly, there was an African American couple who were residents of Portsmouth at the time of the Black Friday exodus who either did not leave or returned after a short time. Their names were Peter and Charlotte Weaver. Peter was the town's first bootblack, making a circuit of the local taverns, shops and other public places every Saturday afternoon to conduct his business. He also worked as an attaché to the courthouse, performing various duties from running errands to digging graves.

However, that was not all that set him apart from the African American community. "Peter Weaver was a member of the First Presbyterian church and prided himself on the fact," Evans stated. "The colored churches did not suit him."[392] This special status may have been what spared him from the full brunt of the community's racial animosity.

Charlotte, described as a "character" by Evans, also seems to have been protected. Born a slave, she was taken by her master, a man named Walker, to Kentucky where she met and married another slave, Peter. After buying his own freedom, Peter borrowed $1,000 to purchase Charlotte's as well. But he was unable to come up with the additional money to buy their child.

The couple then moved to Ohio and built a cabin in what would eventually become Portsmouth. Charlotte apparently made herself indispensable, serving as "a midwife and a factotum about the town," Evans wrote. "No child could be born, no woman buried and no social function be given, without her assistance."[393] Peter continued to reside in Portsmouth until his death in 1865, while Charlotte passed away in Columbus in 1883.

Huston Hollow, like many African American pre–Civil War communities, was never more than a collection of family farms. The pioneering black families had such surnames as Cheney, Gilmore, Smith, Williams, Harris, Isley, Hampton, Love and Chavis or Chavois. Andrew Feight wrote that Huston Hollow "often served as the first Underground Railroad stop for fugitive slaves who had crossed the Ohio River at Portsmouth. Here Joseph Love and Dan Lucas, both African American, are said to have been the most active operators, helping move runaway slaves up the Scioto Valley to the next station in Pike County."[394]

21

SHELBY COUNTY

Rumley and Near Port Jefferson

NEAR PORT JEFFERSON (DINSMORE TOWNSHIP)

Rumley was not the first attempt to create a black settlement in Shelby County. Underground Railroad historian Wilber E. Siebert learned about an earlier one from H.C. Roberts:

> *My father's name was James M. Roberts, Welsh nationality, his father being born in Wales. Grandfather Wm. Roberts and my father came to West Liberty, in Champaign Co., in 1814, with 21 of their 60 freed slaves. They left Virginia for the purpose of freeing their slaves, and were driven away from West Liberty on account of Milk sickness. Two or three of the colored people died, and twelve or fourteen of the cattle about 1818. In the spring of 1819 they came to a little town Port Jefferson, Shelby Co., five and a half miles N.E. of Sidney, with four of their negroes, the others had scattered—Jonathan, Daniel, Minerva, and Hannah were the four colored people.[395]*

Located in Salem Township, Port Jefferson, on the Miami and Erie Canal, was originally known as Pratt. "Mr. Roberts has lived to see Salem Township changed from a howling wilderness to a highly cultivated portion of the country," according to a *History of Shelby County, Ohio*.[396] Another county history records that several "colored families" moved into Salem

Township about 1832, "among them were Moses Redman, George Goins, Humphrey Clinton, and Blake Reynolds. The most of the colored families were located in that part of the township that has since been attached to Dinsmore Township."[397]

However, the 1850 census lists only one black or "mulatto" resident, Daniel W. Colendman (or "Colored Man"), who was residing with a white family, the Maxwells. Perhaps he was the same Daniel who arrived with the Roberts family.

RUMLEY (VAN BUREN TOWNSHIP)

Along the old Indian trail that ran from Piqua to Lima, Colonel Amos Evans mapped out the village of Rumley, Van Buren Township, on May 19, 1837. A year later, he sold the first lot to George Goings (or Goins). The second lot was purchased by Joel Weslin (or Wesley) Goings.[398] Together, the brothers owned nearly four hundred acres. The village contained forty-eight lots altogether.

Architectural historian Mary Ann Brown wrote that Rumley "developed in Shelby County along the Hardin-Wapakoneta Road which meanders in a north-south direction and parallels Interstate 75. The village of Rumley… represents the nucleus of this settlement. The black farmers lived about halfway between the towns of Sidney and Wapakoneta on land around present-day Kettlersville, a small German village platted in 1873 after the black people had begun moving away."[399]

Joel and George were "members of the Wappoo Tribe, Casabo Nation, originally in what is now South Carolina."[400] In 1831, Joel married Elizabeth Cole in Guernsey County. (His sister, Mary, was wed to Mashoe Lett the same year.) The brothers came to Shelby County from the Lett Settlement near Zanesville on the border of Muskingum and Guernsey Counties. By 1850, there were black and mixed-race Goings scattered throughout Auglaize, Clermont, Franklin, Gallia, Hamilton, Highland, Jackson and Shelby Counties.

Colonel Evans built the first hewed log house in Rumley, while Joel built the first one of brick. Brickmakers by trade, the Goings brothers built many homes in the vicinity. However, that was not the extent of their enterprise. Stella Harger Wilson recalled that "stage coaches traveling from one city to another stopped there to either rest the horses overnight or trade horses and continue their journey."[401] Being astute businessmen, the Goings brothers decided it was just the place to locate a hotel and livery stable. They also joined with Elias Spray to operate the first gristmill and Chestine Harrison the first sawmill.

"Rumley was the hub of several free black villages founded in the area," Jill Rowe noted. "It was connected to three of them—specifically Carthagena, Wren, and Middle Creek—by extended family."[402] The residents of Rumley intermarried with free blacks in neighboring counties, including those in other settlements. Three churches served Rumley. The first was an African Methodist Episcopal (AME) church built of logs. Close by was a wood-frame Baptist church. Later, the Wesleyan Methodist Church was added near the AME church. There also were three saloons.

In his history of Ohio, Henry Howe wrote that the black residents of Rumley "constitute half the population of the township, and are as prosperous as their white neighbors. Neither are they behind them in religion, morals and intelligence, having churches and schools of their own. Their location, however, is not a good one, the land being too flat and wet."[403]

Rumley was a mere six miles west of New Bremen, the town where in 1846 the Randolph slaves were thwarted in their attempt to disembark from the canalboats that were supposed to carry them to their new home in Mercer County. However, Guy Kelsey, a local businessman, and Joseph Cummins, who had assisted in laying out Pulaski, convened a meeting with area leaders. "As a result, a number of the incoming black families were settled in the Sidney area and were forced to deal with the prejudices of a large community. A number also settled at Rumley."[404] Among them were the Creaths and Dickersons. Others would follow. "In 1854, a group of 34 blacks from Kentucky settled in the area without difficulty," according to Jim Johnson.[405]

Although there was some Underground Railroad traffic through Shelby County, primarily through Sidney, Rumley's involvement seems to have been minimal. However, with the advent of the Civil War in 1861, the relationship between pro- and antislavery factions in the area became more heated. Southern sympathizers found it safer to direct their anger at Ohio's black residents as opposed to the better armed and more organized white. Hoping to avoid trouble, many African American citizens of Rumley left in search of a more peaceful abode.

A correspondent for the *Cincinnati Commericial* visited Rumley and Carthagena in 1867 and came away favorably impressed. Having been told that the African Americans who lived there were lazy and shiftless, he

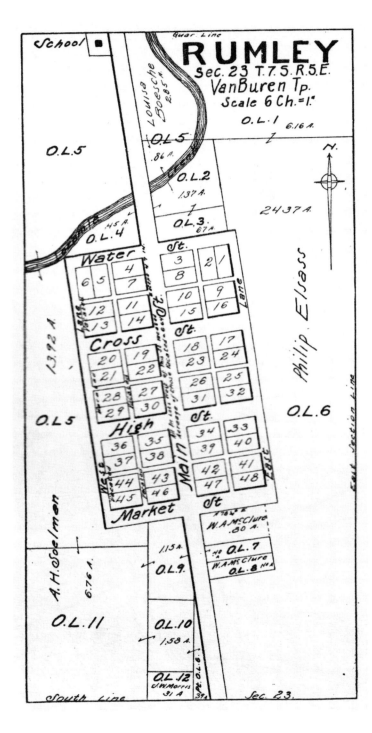

Colonel Amos Evans filed the paperwork, but the Goings brothers may have laid out the town. *Authors' collection.*

learned instead that "the majority more than live by the culture of their farms, that in all years of fair crops they increase in wordly gear and the goods of life."[406] Their homes were modest, clean and well maintained, while their smokehouses were "rejoicing in plenty, and their barns bursting with abundance."[407] The writer noted that these farmers were also paying from $50 to $300 a year in taxes for the support of men and agencies from which they received no benefit and by which they were often oppressed. In short, they were doing much better than might be expected given the circumstances under which they were forced to live, denied representation and the right to vote.

At one point, the African American population of Rumley numbered about four hundred, which was roughly half the population of the town. One of the more remarkable citizens of Rumley was D.C. Goings, son of Joel Goings. At the age of twelve, he began to garner attention in the village as a healer. He attended college to study medicine until the age of twenty-two. In 1860, D.C. married Rebecca Fox, daughter of Archibald Fox, a full-blooded American Indian. She also had ties to the Lett, Cole and Randolph families. Dr. Goings is said to have published a work titled *Faith Healing for the Invalid* in 1900.

Rumley Baptist Church was formerly the Lewis Chapel AME Church. *Author photo.*

The school in Rumley was built on the site of the former Wesleyan Methodist Church. *Author photo.*

Among the most prominent black surnames were Adams, Austin, Bishop, Bond, Boydston, Clinton, Collins, Cook, Copeland, Davis, Farrow, Galloway, Goings (or Gaings), Grant, Jackson, King, Lett, Lucas, Madison, Mason, Redman, Reynolds, Robertson, Rosecrans, Sherman, Stogland, Stuart, Williams and Winslow. In the years that followed, Rumley, like many of the black settlements, experienced more attrition as the farmers failed to make the necessary investment in machinery and methods to keep pace with the competition. During the 1930s, Rumley disappeared entirely.

STARK COUNTY

New Guinea or Lexington

New Guinea or Lexington (Lexington Township)

A brief history of Lexington Township stated:

> *Lexington Township is...the location of the first African American settlement in Stark County. The settlement, called New Guinea, was established along the banks of the Mahoning River about a mile east of Williamsport, the later settlement being located near the site of the old Alliance waterworks. New Guinea, which flourished around 1810, was made up of about 200 freed and runaway slaves who were befriended by the early Quaker settlers in the area. No traces remain of this settlement.*[408]

The name, New Guinea, was a derogatory one. It was never used by those who lived there. Originally located in Columbiana County, it became part of Stark County when the boundaries shifted.

In the life and reminiscences of Ohio poet Elizabeth Shreve-Chambers, there is passing mention of how the community came into existence. In 1805,

> *several families of Friends left the State of Virginia because they were not willing to live in a slave state. They migrated to Lexington township, Stark county, and were its first settlers. This led to an influx of free negroes from Virginia and there were a few who were still claimed as slaves by slaveholders in the south who, from time to time were hunting on their trail.*

The colored people were befriended and aided by the Friends, often times at great sacrifice and risk.[409]

Calling themselves Christ's Disciples, this band of African Americans made their home in an area that was later absorbed by the city of Alliance. "The community was an orderly and industrious one," according to anthropologist Jill Rowe. "There was a school taught by Esther Wileman, a Quakeress, who boarded with one of the families in the community."[410]

By 1827, the community was reported to be in decline as the residents moved to the Michigan or Canada (some sources say Defiance) for the sake of their own safety. However, ten years later, a visiting Quaker indicated it had grown to a "settlement of 51 families numbering 264 individuals."[411] It had two schools, a meetinghouse and a library of 120 books.

As might be expected, facts regarding New Guinea are hard to come by, given the passage of time and its brief existence. Various scholars have recently attempted to piece it together, particularly Debra E. Robinson. In 1949, the Stark County Historical Society published the transcript of a radio script that alluded to its demise: "The Negro settlement, church and burial ground long ago passed into oblivion. The cemetery was plowed under, but in recent years, when repairing the road east of Williamsport, old coffins were dug up, supposed old Negro coffins, looking like old fashioned ironing boards."[412]

Among the original landowners in what became Alliance were Solomon and Julia Day and David and Margaret Day from Virginia. They settled in the middle of the community of New Guinea, although they arrived in 1823 and New Guinea purportedly had already "peaked" at two hundred people in 1810. Yet there is no evidence of a decline in the number of black farmers living in Lexington Township between 1823 and 1840.

"In 1827 (when many slaves were supposedly fleeing elsewhere), [David Day] sold fourteen acres to Shaper Whitfield, a fellow Black Virginian from Southampton."[413] Two years later, Day sold some more land, this time to Christ's Disciples, of which Whitfield was a trustee. The African American surnames that appeared in the 1830 census were Day, Whitfield, Huss, Brian, Browser, Barnes, Powell and Copeland.

Robinson noted that Solomon Day lived nearby, but not in the area designated as New Guinea. His wife passed away not long after they moved to Ohio, and in 1828, he married Nancy Ann Barnhill, daughter of a black farmer from Columbiana County. In 1839, they moved to Logan County, Ohio. While it is not known what prompted this move, there were at least four free black settlements in Logan County. And there were Whitfields there, as well.

VAN WERT COUNTY

East of Wren

EAST WREN (WILLSHIRE TOWNSHIP)

Architectural historian Mary Ann Brown wrote about an important black settlement in Van Wert County. Located two miles east of the Indiana state line, "the center of this settlement was the crossroads east of the hamlet of Wren and north of Schumm, a German community."[414] Informally, it was called East Wren.

Like Paulding to the north, Van Wert County was part of the Great Black Swamp. The two major challenges confronting the first settlers were clearing the forests and draining the land, both necessary to prepare the rich soil that lay beneath for farming. Although the town of Willshire was platted in 1822 and designated the county seat, few people settled there during the next ten or fifteen years and little progress was made.

One of the earliest black settlers was William White. Born a slave, he had been trained as a prizefighter by his master "and soon became a scientific boxer, so quick of eye and motion that ere long his best trainer could not stand up before him."[415] His owner eventually pitted him against another fighter who was regarded as the champion of the South; White won the bout by breaking his opponent's shoulder. But he then refused to fight again, declaring he would rather be sent down the river to pick cotton. Instead of punishing him, White's master gave him his freedom and he moved to Willshire Township. White eventually married Nancy Young and

In the late 1800s, Wren fielded a highly regarded black baseball team. *Wren Historical Society.*

"lived to a good age and was never known to do an act that could not be endorsed by his neighbors."[416]

In 1837, while on a tour sponsored by the Ohio Anti-Slavery Society, Augustus Wattles made two separate trips to Van Wert County. "His purpose was to 'lecture to the colored people and teach school.'"[417] Since Willshire was the only town of consequence in the county, Wattles likely spoke there. Among those presumed to have been in attendance were Godfrey Brown and his son, Samuel, who had come from Brown's Settlement in Greene County. Although Godfrey initially bought 120 acres and Samuel 40, their holdings in Van Wert County increased appreciably over the years.

Four years after Samuel's death in 1870, his sons, William (twenty) and James (eighteen), decided to move to Van Wert County to settle on the eighty-acre plot he had left them in his will. With a team of horses and a spring wagon provided by their mother, they set off four years later. "When they reached their destination," Harvey Brown wrote, "the land was covered with timber. They selected a section, cut the timber and built a log cabin house. Another patch of land was used for a garden."[418]

"The land purchased by the black farmers," Mary Ann Brown observed, "lay next to a small reservation deeded to Jean Baptiste Richardville, who was also known by his Indian name, Pechewa."[419] Covering 1,200 acres on

This abandoned house may have been part of the East Wren settlement. *Author photo.*

both sides of the Ohio-Indiana border, it had been set aside by a Miami chief in 1818 under the terms of the Treaty of St. Marys. Upon the chief's death in 1841, the land was divvied up among his descendants, who may have been more accepting of the African Americans than the white settlers had been.

Situated primarily in Willshire Township, but with a few intrusions into Liberty and Harrison, East Wren was twenty-five miles northwest of Carthagena. At the time of the 1850 census, it contained forty-three blacks and "mulattos." At the settlement's peak, Harvey Brown estimated that it encompassed some two thousand acres.

Ruben Williams and his wife, Jemima, were former slaves. After his master whipped his mother, Ruben killed him with an axe and then fled for his life. He may have taken Jemima with him, and they performed their own marriage ceremony on the steps of a church. It is said that he either drowned the dogs that were chasing him or spread pepper to throw them off the track. There is a family legend, according to historian Jim Bowsher, that Jemima accidentally suffocated their child while trying to keep him quiet as they were fleeing. A kindly Quaker fashioned a wax death mask for them as a keepsake.

The black residents of East Wren founded St. Marys African Methodist Episcopal Church in 1843 and later constructed a building to house it. The

Above: East Wren Cemetery was once shared by two churches. *Author photo.*

Right: The wax death mask of the child of Ruben and Jemima Williams. *Jim Bowsher collection.*

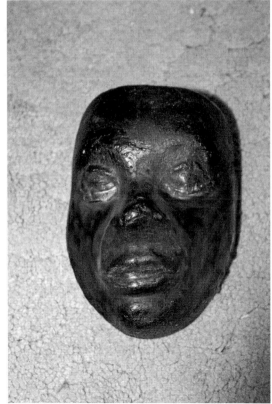

Above: Elizabeth "Libby" Brown Saunders taught Wren's black students at the original brick school. *Wren Historical Society.*
Below: "Chicken Pickers"—both black and white—worked side by side at this Wren company. *Wren Historical Society.*

Educational Orphans Institute was founded ten years later. Brothers William and James Brown helped organize and build Second Zion Baptist Church in 1883. They would each live in houses nearby, one to the north and the other to the south. Although they married sisters—William to Alice Pettiford and James to Belle Pettiford—only William fathered any children.

Many African American males had rushed to enlist in the U.S. military immediately after the fall of Fort Sumter but were turned away. However, the law prohibiting their serving changed in 1862. Those from East Wren who served the Union during the Civil War were Frank and Walter Lewis, Nathan Mitchell, William, John D. and Joseph Updegrove, John D. White, Rueben Williams and Chelsley, George H. and James A. Young. After the war, most of the soldiers returned home, resumed farming and, for the most part, lived in peace with their white neighbors.

While it never was a particularly large community, East Wren held its own well into the first half of the twentieth century. As Mary Ann Brown pointed out, compared to Carthagena and Rumley, the East Wren farms were under black ownership much later, with at least five hundred acres still in their possession in 1900. However, by the 1920s, most of the black residents had moved to the cities in search of work. Now, all that remains is the East Wren Cemetery, which skirts an old railroad bed near the two site of the two churches that shared it.[420] Those buried there include the surnames Brown, Galloway, Green, Hardmon, Mitchell, Nukes, Underwood, Upthegrove, White, Williams and Young.

Skip Young was a farmer in East Wren who played baseball in his spare time. *Wren Historical Society.*

WARREN COUNTY

Harveysburg

HARVEYSBURG (MASSIE TOWNSHIP)

Harveysburg, in Massie Township, Warren County, was about ten miles southwest of Brown's Settlement as the crow flies. Founded by William Harvey in 1829, it was a Quaker community and reflected their values. Realizing that the African American and Native American children in the area were in need of education, Elizabeth Burgess Harvey, wife of Dr. Jesse Harvey, proposed to the members of the Grove Monthly Meeting of Friends that they establish a school. With the ongoing support of the other Quakers, the Harveys built the Harveysburg Free Black School in 1831. It was one of the first institutions for children of color in Ohio.

Hearing of the school, Colonel Stephen Wall, a wealthy plantation owner and politician from North Carolina, decided it would be just the place to send the eight children he had fathered by three different enslaved women.[421] His offspring were Orindatus Simon Bolivar Wall, Caroline Malinda "Carrie" Wall and Benjamin Franklin Wall (all children of Pricilla "Prissy" Ely); Sarah Kelly Wall and Napoleon B. Wall (children of Jane Ely, Priscilla's sister); and John Wall, Albert G. Wall and Peter Wall (children of Rhody or Rhoday).

According to genealogist Karen Campbell, Jane was given her freedom, but Priscilla wasn't. Apparently, there was no love lost between Priscilla and

Quakers in Harveysburg established an early free school for black students. *Author photo.*

Colonel Wall, for she reportedly once said that he should have been "burned at the stake a long time ago."[422] Campbell found no evidence that Peter Wall ever relocated to Ohio.

WYANDOT COUNTY

Negro Town and Sandusky Plains

NEGRO TOWN (TYMOCHTEE TOWNSHIP)

As early as 1811, there was a small settlement called Negro Town in what would become Wyandot County.[423] Nothing is known concerning its founding. James Barton recalled nearly forty years later that when he arrived in the area, it consisted of a group of log huts "inhabited by Indians, except an old Negro called 'Tom' and his family, and a white man named Wright who was married to Tom's daughter."[424]

In 1816, John Stewart, a free-born African American, presented himself to the Wyandots living in the vicinity, intent on preaching the gospel. He soon founded the first church in Upper Sandusky. Two years later, he married Polly Carter, a black resident of Negro Town. According to Larry Hancks, "A 60 acre farm [was] purchased for John and Polly Stewart adjacent to the Wyandots' Grand Reserve with funds raised by Methodist Bishop McKendree."[425] In 1911, a souvenir booklet was published by B.F. Walton in honor of the twenty-six students attending the Negro Town public school.

SANDUSKY PLAINS SETTLEMENT (UNIDENTIFIED TOWNSHIP)

Little is known about the Sandusky Plains Settlement. Even its location is a mystery.[426] The Sandusky Plains once spread across Wyandot, Marion and Crawford Counties.

It is in Crawford County that the vast prairies prevailing in Western States are first made manifest. A large one, about thirty miles long, and having an average width of five or six miles, begins in northeastern Whetstone Township, extending southwestwardly across Buoyrus and Dallas Townships, far down into Marion County.[427]

In his brief account of this particular band of former Gist slaves, Philip Schwarz stated, "Still another contingent of people was sent to northern Ohio in the Sandusky District, on the Sandusky Plains, south of Upper Sandusky."[428] This would place it near the Killdeer Plains Wildlife Area in Wyandot County. "A crop was prepared for them in advance so they would not suffer as had the Brown County settlers," Schwarz noted, "but they left this Sandusky Plains settlement as quickly as they had arrived."[429]

According to stories passed down through the generations, the settlers, some 120 in number, "were dissatisfied because of the climate, the malaria, and the mosquitoes, and they walked their homesick ways back to 'Ole Virginny.'"[430] But there was apparently another, more urgent reason: the white settlers, fearing they might intermarry with their children, gave them fifteen days to leave or they would "set the [Wyandot] Indians on them."[431] In 1843, the Wyandots were the last tribe to leave Ohio. Before that, they

By 1900, resentment began to build against black residents due to their large families. *Jean Miller.*

had withdrawn to the area of Upper Sandusky, which would become the county seat five years after they had departed.

A dozen years after the Sandusky Plains group returned to Virginia, they were purportedly relocated to Adams and Highland Counties. The trustees had taken their time, not wanting to risk another failure, even though there was a chance of re-enslavement while they remained in Virginia.

Notes

Introduction

1. Gannon, "Race Is a Social Construct, Scientists Argue."
2. Thomas, "Where Are the Randolphs."

Prologue

3. Middleton, *Black Laws*.
4. "The Randolph Slaves," *Richmond (VA) Enquirer*, July 24, 1846.
5. Ibid.
6. Ibid.
7. "The Randolph Slaves," *Daily Union* (Washington, D.C.), July 17, 1846.

Chapter 1

8. Free African Americans, "Virginia Slaves Freed After 1782."
9. Wolfe, *Stories of Guernsey County*.
10. Ibid.
11. Ibid.
12. Caldwell, *History of Belmont and Jefferson Counties*.
13. "Captina African Methodist Episcopal Church Cemetery Restoration Remembered during Black History," *Barnesville (OH) Enterprise*, February 22, 2017.
14. Ibid.
15. "Old Settler Family Pages," oldsettlersreunion.com, accessed January 10, 2019.

Chapter 2

16. Galbreath, "Anti-Slavery Movement in Columbiana County."
17. Evans and Stivers, *History of Adams County.*
18. Birney, *James G. Birney and His Times.*
19. Crawford, *Samuel Doak.*
20. Rankin, who was born in Jefferson County, Tennessee, moved to Ripley, Ohio, in 1821, and assumed a leading role in the Underground Railroad.
21. *History of Brown County, Ohio.*
22. Schwarz, *Migrants Against Slavery.*
23. Toler was one of the surnames adopted by the Gist slaves.
24. *Acts Passed at a General Assembly of the Commonwealth of Virginia.*
25. Schwarz, *Migrants Against Slavery.*
26. Turner, "Gist Settlement Keeps Alive Days of Long Ago."
27. Munford, *Virginia's Attitude Toward Slavery.*
28. *History of Brown County, Ohio.*
29. Ibid.
30. Ibid.
31. Letter from Paul Tomlinson, Cedarville, Ohio, to Siebert, March 21, 1895.
32. Schwarz, *Migrants Against Slavery.*
33. *Cincinnati (OH) Enquirer*, "Charles Hammond on Free Negroes," April 5, 1865.
34. Ibid.
35. Ibid.
36. Schwarz, *Migrants Against Slavery.*
37. Powell, Kavanaugh and Christy, "Transplanting Free Negroes to Ohio."
38. Munford, *Virginia's Attitude Toward Slavery.*
39. *Maumee (OH) City Express*, "Self Defence," June 8, 1839.
40. Ibid.
41. *Portsmouth (OH) Daily Times*, "Emancipation and Its Results," June 21, 1862.
42. Letter from Paul Tomlinson, Cedarville, Ohio, to Siebert, March 21, 1895.
43. Wright, "Negro Rural Communities in Indiana."
44. Ibid.

Chapter 3

45. Middleton, *History of Champaign County.*
46. Ibid.
47. Ibid.
48. Ibid.
49. GENi, "Abraham Van Meter: Will."
50. Ibid.
51. Dr. Gates has not been able to discover why his ancestors happened to choose the Bruce surname.
52. African American Lives, "Who Am I? A Genealogy Guide."

53. Abraham Vanmeter is easily confused with his nephew of the same name who is an heir in his will.
54. ArcGIS Online, "Tracking Freedom."

Chapter 4

55. Miller, *Palestine Book.*
56. National Park Service, "James & Sophia Clemens Farmstead."
57. DuBois, "Long in Darke."
58. Ibid.
59. Ibid.
60. McRae, "Bass and Clemens Cemeteries in Darke County, Ohio."
61. Goins and variations thereof is the most widespread surname found in tri-racial groups.
62. DuBois, "Long in Darke."
63. Ibid.
64. Tucker, *History of Randolph County.*
65. Ibid.
66. DuBois, "Long in Darke."
67. Ibid.
68. Ibid.
69. It is one of several communities in Ohio regarded as tri-racial, including the so-called Carmel Indians of Highland County, the Vinton County Indians in Jackson/Vinton County, the Saponi Nation of Ohio in Gallia County and the Guineas in southeastern Ohio.

Chapter 5

70. Thomas Jefferson wrote in 1814, "The laws do not permit us to turn [our slaves] loose," *Jefferson Monticello.* https://www.monticello.org/site/plantation-and-slavery/living-free-virginia. Accessed September 31, 2019.
71. UNC Greensboro, "Petition 11483106 Details."
72. Twenty-nine white men signed his petition, attesting to his good character.
73. Woodson, *Journal of Negro History.*
74. Perrin, *History of Delaware County.*
75. Ibid.
76. Woodson, *Journal of Negro History.*
77. In 1938, Poindexter Village, a public housing project in Columbus, was named in his honor.
78. Lytle, *Twentieth Century History of Delaware County,*
79. Allen, "He Built His Own Resort."
80. Ibid.
81. In 1873, Lucy married Thomas A. Whyte, a farmer and blacksmith, who was the son of Dr. Samuel W. Whyte.

82. Allen, "He Built His Own Resort."
83. Ibid.
84. Albrecht, "Neighborhood Not What It Used to Be."
85. Allen, "He Built His Own Resort."
86. Perrin, *History of Delaware County*.
87. Hunt, "History of 'Africa.'"
88. Ibid.
89. Ibid.
90. Lytle, "Alston Freed Slaves."
91. Ibid.
92. Ibid.
93. Ibid.
94. Hunt, "History of 'Africa.'"
95. Ibid.
96. Ibid.

Chapter 6

97. Averill, *History of Gallia County*.
98. Ibid.
99. Martzloff, *Brief History of Athens County*.
100. Ibid.
101. Welcome to the Lawrence County Register, "Poke Patch History."
102. J. Willard Marriott Library, "Hood, Frances Ann Stewart."
103. LaRoche, *Free Black Communities*.
104. "Lambert Land," *Gallia (OH) Herald*, November 3, 2013.
105. Inscoe, *Appalachians and Race*.
106. "The Lambert Land Settlement," Remarkable Ohio.
107. "Lambert Land."
108. Waldron, "Lambert Lands…Settlement for Slaves."
109. Ibid.
110. Price, "Memorial Honors Lambert Settlers."
111. Waldron, "Lambert Lands…Settlement for Slaves."
112. Ibid.
113. Price, "Memorial Honors Lambert Settlers."
114. "Lambert Land."

Chapter 7

115. Robinson, *History of Greene County*.
116. "Freed Negroes of Early Days," *Xenia (OH) Daily Gazette*, February 6, 1936.
117. Sarah was the daughter of Peter Pelham, the first auditor of Greene County.
118. *Xenia (OH) Daily News*, July 30, 1900.

119. Brown, *Descendants of Godfrey Brown, Sr.*
120. Baxter, "Godfrey Brown Builds a Church."
121. Brown, *Descendants of Godfrey Brown, Sr.*
122. Ibid.
123. *Cincinnati Journal of Homoeopathy.*
124. "A Black Watering Place," *Evening Star*, August 14, 1854.
125. Ibid.
126. *(Buffalo, NY) Advocate*, October 30, 1856.
127. In 1844, Payne had opened the Union Seminary in Franklin County near West Jefferson, Ohio, under the auspices of the Ohio Conference of the African Methodist Episcopal Church. It would merge with Wilberforce University.
128. Wright, "Negro Rural Communities in Indiana."
129. "Deed Volume 32 page 188," accessed March 9, 2019.
130. Ibid.
131. Heise, "From Mississippi to Greene County Ohio."
132. Ibid.
133. The present-day value of Piper's $36,000 in holdings would exceed $1 million.
134. Wright, "Negro Rural Communities in Indiana."
135. Washington, *Story of the Negro.*
136. Dills, *History of Greene County.*
137. Conway, *Testimonies Concerning Slavery.*
138. Ibid.
139. Ibid.
140. "A Rich Colored Man Dead," *Salem (OH) Daily News*, May 12, 1894.
141. Conway, *Autobiography.*
142. Ibid.
143. Robinson, "The Negro in the Village of Yellow Springs."

Chapter 8

144. Schwarz, *Migrants Against Slavery.*
145. Turner, "Gist Settlement Keeps Alive Days of Long Ago."
146. Richards, "Gist Settlement."
147. *Acts of a Local Nature Passed by the Forty-Ninth General Assembly of the State of Ohio.* Columbus OH: S. Medary, 1851.
148. Ibid.
149. Schwarz, *Migrants Against Slavery.*
150. Ibid.
151. Scott, *History of the Early Settlement of Highland County.*
152. Turner, "Gist Settlement Keeps Alive Days of Long Ago."
153. Williams, "Slavery's Long Legacy in a Corner of Ohio."
154. Ibid.

Chapter 9

155. "Old Settler Family Pages."
156. Ibid.
157. Massie, "Payne Cemetery."
158. Ibid.
159. Ibid.
160. "The Old Settlers: A Nation within Mecosta," oldsettlersreunion.com.
161. "Old Settler Family Pages."
162. "Old Settlers: A Nation within Mecosta."
163. Massie, "Riddles of the Past."

Chapter 10

164. Stevens, "District's Woodson Family."
165. Although the oral tradition is compelling, a 1998 DNA study does not support Woodson being Jefferson's son.
166. Setlock, "Thomas Jefferson and Sally Hemings."
167. Calarco, *Search for the Underground Railroad.*
168. History of American Women, "Sarah Jane Woodson Early."
169. The actual town of Berlin Cross Roads was platted by Charles Kinnison in 1842.
170. LaRoche, *Free Black Communities.*
171. Calarco, *Search for the Underground Railroad.*
172. Stevens, "District's Woodson Family."
173. Ibid.
174. History of American Women, "Sarah Jane Woodson Early."
175. Ibid.
176. Ibid.
177. Letter from J.J. Minor Sr., Portsmouth, Ohio, to W.H. Siebert, September 1894.
178. "Editors," *Jackson (OH) Standard*, February 9, 1855.
179. Vega, "Part III: The DNA Trail from Madagascar to Virginia."
180. Ibid.
181. Ibid.
182. Meghan Markle, wife of Prince Harry, is descended from the Raglands through her mother, Doria.
183. Antipodean, "Distributed A/C Book for William Ragland's Negroes."
184. Ibid.
185. *History of Lower Scioto Valley*, 1884.
186. "Roots and the New 'Faction,'" *Virginia Magazine of History.*
187. "Notice," *Jackson (OH) Standard*, September 6, 1866.
188. Ervin, "Memories of Big Rock Shared."

Chapter 11

189. *History of the Upper Ohio Valley*, 1890.
190. Benford may have been the anglicized version of Beaufort, an old French name
191. It has been claimed that Benjamin Ladd purchased fifty acres of land near Sandusky in 1821 and attempted to settle four hundred African Americans there, but they were soon driven away. This may be a conflation with the rumored Gist Settlement on the Sandusky Plains.
192. Hunter, "Pathfinders of Jefferson County."
193. Powell, Kavanaugh and Christie, "Transplanting Free Negroes to Ohio."
194. Ibid.
195. Hunter, "Pathfinders of Jefferson County."
196. Ibid.
197. Ibid.
198. Powell, Kavanaugh and Christie, "Transplanting Free Negroes to Ohio."
199. Hunter, "Pathfinders of Jefferson County."
200. Ibid.
201. Ibid.
202. Ibid.
203. Powell, Kavanaugh and Christie, "Transplanting Free Negroes to Ohio."
204. Hunter, "Pathfinders of Jefferson County."
205. Defrank, *Times Leader* (Martins Ferry, OH), February 25, 2018.
206. "Emancipation," *Triweekly Washington (D.C.) Sentinel*, October 13, 1855.
207. "Slaves Emancipated," *Pittsburgh Gazette*, October 20, 1855.
208. Defrank, *Times Leader* (Martins Ferry, OH), February 25, 2018.
209. "Prefer Slavery," *Cadiz (OH) Democratic Sentinel*, Mary 28, 1857.
210. Defrank, *Times Leader* (Martins Ferry, OH), February 25, 2018.

Chapter 12

211. *Atlas of Lawrence County*, 1887.
212. Malloy, "Students Tell Blackfork Story."
213. RootsWeb, "Brenda Keck Reed's Kith & Kin."
214. Ibid.
215. Ibid.
216. "Blacks and Mulattoes," *Ohio State Journal and Columbus (OH) Gazette*, May 3, 1827.
217. Ibid.
218. UNC Greensboro, Race & Slavery Petitions Project.
219. Ross and Breeden, "Freed Madison Slaves Leave Lasting Legacy."
220. Ibid.
221. Wilson, "Old Times."
222. Calarco, *Places of the Underground Railroad*.
223. Malloy, "Man Says Church in Lawrence Was Underground Railroad Stop."

224. "Division of Property of the Emancipated Slaves of James Twyman," *Ironton (OH) Register*, September 22, 1870.
225. "Copperhead Church Movement," *Chicago Daily Tribune*, March 27, 1864.
226. Ibid.
227. Ibid.
228. Ibid.
229. "Sudden Death," *Ironton (OH) Register*, October 11, 1888.
230. Willard, *Standard History of the Hanging Rock Region*.
231. Gabe N. Johnson interview with Wilbur Siebert, September 30, 1894..
232. LaRoche, *Free Black Communities*.

Chapter 13

233. Perrin and Battle, *History of Logan County*.
234. Ibid.
235. Ibid.
236. Ibid.
237. Library of Virginia, "John Warwick."
238. Ibid.
239. Ibid.
240. Ibid.
241. "Manumission of Slaves," *Anti-Slavery Bugle* (Lisbon, OH), April 28, 1848.
242. Munford, *Virginia's Attitude Toward Slavery*.
243. Perrin and Battle, *History of Logan County*.
244. Ibid.
245. Love, "Registration of Free Blacks in Ohio."
246. Perrin and Battle, *History of Logan County*.
247. Ibid.
248. Ibid.
249. NCpedia, "Newlin, John."
250. Ibid.
251. AfriGeneas, "AfriGeneas Genealogy and History Forum."
252. Perrin and Battle, *History of Logan County*.
253. Meyers and Walker, *Lynching and Mob Violence in Ohio*.
254. Browning, "G.C. Mendenhall Had Slaves."
255. Stockard, *History of Guilford County*.
256. Browning, "G.C. Mendenhall Had Slaves."
257. Love, "Registration of Free Blacks in Ohio."
258. Ibid.
259. Ibid.
260. Browning, "G.C. Mendenhall Had Slaves."
261. Drumbolis, *Wayward Letters*.
262. Browning, "G.C. Mendenhall Had Slaves."

Chapter 14

263. Brown, "Vanished Black Rural Communities."

264. Woodson, *Century of Negro Migration*.

265. Muller, *Red, Black and White*.

266. Howe, *Historical Collections of Ohio*.

267. Woodson, *Century of Negro Migration*.

268. Rowe, *Invisible in Plain Sight*.

269. "Colored Settlement," *Pittsburgh Gazette*, December 2, 1840.

270. Muller, *Red, Black and White*.

271. Although there is no question that Charles bought the land in Marion Township that became Carthagena, Dorcas actually laid out the town according to Nicey Moore, a descendant.

272. Scranton, *History of Mercer County*.

273. Cox, *Bone and Sinew*.

274. The son of a prominent Quaker minister, Emlen and his wife had moved from Philadelphia to New Jersey to escape the yellow fever epidemic. He was a widower and had no children.

275. Woodson, *Century of Negro Migration*.

276. The Emlen Institute was relocated to Solebury, Pennsylvania, and then to Warminster Township, eventually forming the nucleus of Cheyney State University.

277. In 1955, Wattles would move to Kansas, where he became a close friend of John Brown, the abolitionist. He even joined a plan to break Brown out of jail.

278. Ibid.

279. Ibid.

280. Ibid.

281. Ibid.

282. *History of Van Wert and Mercer Counties*, 1882.

283. "Colored Farmers in Ohio," *Highland (County, OH) Weekly News*, August 2, 1867, 2.

284. There are twelve chapters dealing with life in Carthagena. McCray and McCray, *Life of Mary Francis McCray*.

285. Newkirk, *Letters from Black America*.

286. Ibid.

287. Ibid.

288. Ibid.

289. Ibid.

290. Ibid.

Chapter 15

291. Rayner, *First Century of Piqua*.

292. "John Randolph's Slaves," *Wyandotte (KS) Gazette*, June 21, 1878.

293. Ibid.

294. Ibid.

295. "Correspondence of the Morning Herald," *Anti-Slavery Bugle* (Lisbon, OH), August 21, 1846.

296. Ibid.

297. Ibid.

298. "Former Slave of Randolph Dies in Piqua," *Piqua (OH) Daily Call*, December 22, 1903.

299. "John Randolph's Slaves," *Wyandotte (KS) Gazette*.

300. Ibid.

301. Ibid.

302. "Blind Negro, Age 81, Tells Vividly of Early Slave Days," *Piqua (OH) Daily Call*, July 14, 1923.

303. "Randolph's Slaves," *Portage (County, OH) Sentinel*, August 12, 1846.

304. "John Randolph's Slaves," *Portage (County, OH) Sentinel*, December 9, 1846.

305. "John Randolph's Slaves," *Wyandotte (KS) Gazette*.

306. Hover, *Memoirs of the Miami Valley*.

307. Porcher, "Who Were the Randolph Slaves?"

308. Ohio History Connection, "Settling Rossville."

309. "Only a Very Few of Them Now Living," *Dayton (OH) Daily News*, January 18, 1913.

310. Honeyman, "Hanktown Community."

311. Ibid.

312. Porcher, "Who Were the Randolph Slaves?"

313. Ibid.

314. Honeyman, "Hanktown Community."

Chapter 16

315. Old Settlers Reunion Association, "Lett Families Settlement History & Genealogy."

316. Ibid.

317. "Colored Citizens' News," *Times Recorder* (Zanesville, OH), September 25, 1925.

318. Everhart, *History of Muskingum County*.

319. Ibid.

320. Ibid.

321. "Question of Color," *Richmond (VA) Dispatch*, December 21, 1867.

322. Everhart, *History of Muskingum County*.

323. Ibid.

324. Colored Conventions.

325. Everhart, *History of Muskingum County*.

326. "Question of Color."

Chapter 17

327. Howe, *Historical Collections of Ohio.*
328. Brown, "Vanished Black Rural Communities."
329. UNC Greensboro, Race & Slavery Petitions Project.
330. Ibid.
331. "Slaves Emancipated!" *Vermont Telegraph,* June 10, 1840.
332. Ibid.
333. Morrow and Bashore, *Historical Atlas of Paulding County.*
334. Ibid.
335. Gusler, *Partial History of the Gusler Family.*
336. Morrow and Bashore, *Historical Atlas of Paulding County.*
337. Ibid.
338. Federal Writers' Project, "Slave Narratives."
339. Turley, "Spirited Away."
340. Rowe, "Mixing it Up."
341. Hughes and Sullivan, *Hughes Family of Kentucky and Virginia.*
342. Ibid.
343. Rowe, *Invisible in Plain Sight.*
344. Morrow and Bashore, *Historical Atlas of Paulding County.*

Chapter 18

345. One source said in was the "Downings" who had it written into the document, but there is no evidence they had anything to do with the courthouse. Homepage of James W. Loewen, "Showing Waverly in OH."
346. Howe, *Historical Collections of Ohio.*
347. *History of Lower Scioto Valley,* 1884.
348. Howe, *Historical Collections of Ohio.*
349. Schrader, "Historical Study of the Negro."
350. Dippel, *Race to the Frontier.*
351. Ibid.
352. Ibid.
353. "Life among the Lowly: Number II," *Pike County (OH) Republican,* November 20, 1873.
354. Ibid.
355. Ibid.
356. Ibid.
357. Ibid.
358. Ibid.
359. Ibid.
360. Ibid.
361. *History of Lower Scioto Valley,* 1884.
362. Black/Land Project, "When Place Makes Race."

363. State of the Re:Union, "Pike County, OH."
364. Howe, *Historical Collections of Ohio*.
365. Meyers and Walker, *Lynching and Mob Violence in Ohio*.
366. Gray, "Eden Baptist Church."
367. Ohio History Central, "Eden Baptist Church."
368. "Life among the Lowly, No. 1," *Pike County (OH) Republican*, March 13, 1873.
369. Ibid.
370. Jefferson kept his promise regarding their children but did not free Sally. She would die a slave.
371. Although Jefferson would list Beverly and Harriet as "run" (i.e., escaped), evidence points to the fact that he allowed them to leave.
372. "Life among the Lowly, No. 3," *Pike County (OH) Republican*, December 25, 1897.
373. Ibid.
374. Ibid.
375. Ibid.

Chapter 19

376. Finley and Putnam, *Pioneer Record and Reminiscences*.
377. Salafia, *Slavery's Borderland*.
378. UNC Greensboro, "Slave Ownership History."
379. Lednum, *History of the Rise of Methodism*.
380. Bennett, *County of Ross*.
381. Morgan, *Rise and Progress*.
382. Ibid.
383. Langston, *From the Virginia Plantation*.
384. Ibid.
385. Samuel Cox would go on to become the principal of Chillicothe's black schools.
386. Langston, *From the Virginia Plantation*.
387. Bennett, *County of Ross*.
388. Turpin, *Register of Black, Mulatto and Poor Families*.
389. Simmons, *Men of Mark*.

Chapter 20

390. Meyers and Walker, *Lynching and Mob Violence in Ohio*.
391. Feight, "Black Friday."
392. Evans, *History of Scioto County*.
393. Ibid.
394. Feight, "'Black Friday.'"

Chapter 21

395. Interview with H.C. Roberts by W.H. Siebert, July 5, 1895.
396. *History of Shelby County*, 1883.
397. Ibid.
398. Some sources say that the Goings brothers actually platted Rumley, although Evans registered it at the courthouse.
399. Brown, "Vanished Black Rural Communities."
400. Rowe, "Mixing It Up."
401. Wilson and Nelson, *Centennial History of Rumley*.
402. Rowe, *Invisible in Plain Sight*.
403. Howe, *Historical Collections of Ohio*.
404. Johnson, "Shelby County's Black History Rooted in Virginia."
405. Ibid.
406. "The Colored Farmers of Ohio," *Highland (County, OH) Weekly News*, August 22, 1867.
407. Ibid.

Chapter 22

408. Lexington Township, "History of Lexington Township."
409. Shreve, *Poems of Elizabeth Shreve-Chambers*.
410. Rowe, "In Strength & Struggle."
411. Cox, *Bone and Sinew*.
412. Robinson, *Purgatory between Kentucky and Canada*.
413. Ibid.

Chapter 23

414. Brown, "Vanished Black Rural Communities."
415. Gilliland, *History of Van Wert County*.
416. Ibid.
417. Rowe, *Invisible in Plain Sight*.
418. Find A Grave, "William Harvey Brown."
419. Brown, "Vanished Black Rural Communities."
420. Also known as St. Marys Cemetery and Youngs Colored Cemetery.

Chapter 24

421. These were, by definition, involuntary relationships.
422. Campbell, "Captain Ordinatus Simon Bolivar Wall."

Chapter 25

423. Old Northwest Notebook, "Unfinished Story of Negro Town."

424. "Address by James L. Barton," *Buffalo (NY) Commercial*, March 1, 1848.

425. Hancks, "Emigrant Tribes."

426. Some historians have placed the settlement in Erie County, Ohio, near the city of Sandusky.

427. *History of Crawford County*, 1881.

428. Schwarz, *Migrants Against Slavery*.

429. Ibid.

430. Turner, "Gist Settlement Keeps Alive Days of Long Ago."

431. Schwarz, *Migrants Against Slavery*.

BIBLIOGRAPHY

Books

Acts of a Local Nature Passed by the Forty-Ninth General Assembly of the State of Ohio. Columbus, OH: S. Medary, 1851.

Acts Passed at a General Assembly of the Commonwealth of Virginia. Richmond, VA: Thomas Ritchie, 1816.

Atlas of Lawrence County, Ohio. Chicago: H.H. Hardesty & Company, 1882; Philadelphia, PA. D.J. Lake & Company, 1887.

Averill, James P. *History of Gallia County.* Chicago: H.H. Hardesty & Company, 1882.

Bennett, Henry Holcomb, ed. *The County of Ross.* Madison, WI: Slevyn A. Brant, 1902.

Birney, William. *James G. Birney and His Times.* New York: D. Appleton and Company, 1890.

Brown, Harvey Arthur. *Descendants of Godfrey Brown, Sr.* Fort Wayne, IN: Allen County Public Library, 1955.

Calarco, Tom. *Places of the Underground Railroad.* Santa Barbara, CA: Greenwood, 2011.

———. *Search for the Underground Railroad in South-Central Ohio.* Charleston, SC: The History Press, 2018.

Caldwell, J.A. *History of Belmont and Jefferson Counties, Ohio.* Wheeling, WV: Historical Publishing Company, 1880.

Clement, Maud Carter. *The History of Pittsylvania County, Virginia.* Baltimore, MD: Clearfield Company, 1987.

Conway, Moncure Daniel. *Autobiography: Memories and Experiences of Moncure Daniel Conway.* Vol. 2. New York: Cassell and Company, 1904.

———. *Testimonies Concerning Slavery.* London: Chapman and Hall, 1864.

Cox, Anna-Lisa. *The Bone and Sinew of the Land.* New York: Public Affairs, 2018.

Crawford, Earle W. *Samuel Doak: Pioneer Missionary of East Tennessee.* Johnson City, TN: Overmountain Press, 1999.

Dills, R.S. *History of Greene County, Ohio*. Dayton, OH: Odell & Mayer, 1881.

Dippel, John V.H. *Race to the Frontier*. New York: Algora Publishing, 2005.

Drumbolis, Nick. *Wayward Letters: Clues to the Disappearance of Louise Palmer Heaven*. https://archive.org/details/rthrcravan_gmail_LPHX/page/n3.

Etheridge, Lesley Gist, ed. *They Followed the North Star to Gist Settlement, 1810–1985*. New Vienna, OH: First Presbyterian Church, 2005.

Evans, Lyle S., ed. *A Standard History of Ross County, Ohio*. Chicago: Lewis Publishing, 1917.

Evans, Nelson W. *A History of Scioto County, Ohio*. Portsmouth, OH: Nelson W. Evans, 1903.

Evans, Nelson W., and Emmons B. Stivers. *A History of Adams County, Ohio*. West Union, OH: K.B. Stivers, 1900.

Everhart, J.F. *History of Muskingum County, Ohio*. Columbus, OH: J.F. Everhart & Company, 1882.

Finley, Isaac J., and Rufus Putnam. *Pioneer Record and Reminiscences of the Early Settlers and Settlement of Ross County, Ohio*. Cincinnati, OH: Clarke & Clarke, 1871.

Gehres, Marlin. *District of Greenwood to Wren, 1883–1976*. Rockford, OH: Wren Historical Society, 1976.

Gilliland, Thaddeus S. *History of Van Wert County, Ohio*. Chicago: Richmond & Arnold, 1906.

Gusler, Gilbert. *A Partial History of the Gusler Family*. Self-published, 1954. Internet Archive. https://openlibrary.org/works/OL7500614W/A_partial_history_of_the_Gusler_(Gossler)_family. Accessed July 1, 2019.

Hipp, Laurence R. *History of Grover Hill*. Grover Hill, OH: Laurence R. Hipp, 1971.

The History of Brown County, Ohio. Chicago: W.H. Beers & Company, 1883.

History of Crawford County, Ohio. Chicago: Baskin & Battey, 1881

History of Lower Scioto Valley, Ohio. Chicago: Inter-State Publishing Company, 1884.

History of Shelby County, Ohio. Philadelphia, PA: R. Sutton & Company, 1883.

History of the Upper Ohio Valley. Madison, WI: Brant & Fuller, 1890.

History of Van Wert and Mercer Counties, Ohio. Wapakoneta, OH: R. Sutton & Company, 1882.

Hover, John Calvin, et al, eds. *Memoirs of the Miami Valley*. Chicago: Robert O. Law Company, 1919.

Howe, Henry. *Historical Collections of Ohio*. Cincinnati, OH: C.J. Krehbiel & Company, 1907.

Hughes, Lydia Annie, and Richard Hughes Sullivan. *Hughes Family of Kentucky and Virginia*. Columbia, SC: McCaw of Columbia, 1921.

Inscoe, John C., ed. *Appalachians and Race*. Lexington: University of Kentucky Press, 2011.

Jones, Rufus M. *The Later Periods of Quakerism*. London: MacMillan and Company, 1921.

Langston, John Mercer. *From the Virginia Plantation to the National Capitol*. Hartford, CT: American Publishing, 1894.

LaRoche, Cheryl Janifer. *Free Black Communities and the Underground Railroad*. Urbana: University of Illinois Press, 2014.

Lednum, John. *A History of the Rise of Methodism in American*. Philadelphia, PA: self-published, 1859.

Lytle, A.R. *Twentieth Century History of Delaware County Ohio*. Chicago: Biographical Publishing, 1908.

Martzloff, Clement L. *A Brief History of Athens County, Ohio*. Athens, OH: self-published, 1916.

McCray, Sandy J., and Prince McCray. *Life of Mary Francis McCray*. Lima, OH: self-published, 1898.

Meyers, David, and Elise Meyers Walker. *Lynching and Mob Violence in Ohio, 1772–1938*. Jefferson, NC: McFarland & Company Inc., 2019.

Middleton, Evan P. *History of Champaign County, Ohio*. Indianapolis, IN: B.F. Bowen & Company, 1917.

Middleton, Stephen. *The Black Laws: Race and the Legal Process in Early Ohio*. Athens: Ohio University Press, 2005.

Miller, Steven J. *The Palestine Book: History of Liberty (German) Township, Darke County, Ohio*. Greenville, OH: Self-published, 1983.

Morgan, J.B.F. *The Rise and Progress of the Deer Creek Settlement*. Manuscript, 1889. http://jwmyers3.com/family/Book-DeerCreekSettlement/Book-DeerCreekSettlement.html. Accessed March 3, 2019.

Morrow, O., and F.W. Bashore. *Historical Atlas of Paulding County, Ohio*. Madison, WI: Western Publishing, 1892.

Muller, Ulrich F. *Red, Black and White*. Carthagena, OH: Self-published, 1935.

Munford, Beverly Bland. *Virginia's Attitude Toward Slavery and Secession*. New York: Longmans, Green and Company, 1909.

Newkirk, Pamela. *Letters from Black America*. New York: Farrar, Straus and Giroux, 2009.

Perrin, William Henry. *History of Delaware County and Ohio*. Chicago: O.L. Baskin & Company, 1880.

Perrin, W.H., and J.H. Battle. *History of Logan County, Ohio*. Chicago: O.L. Baskin & Company, 1880.

Rayner, John A. *The First Century of Piqua, Ohio*. Piqua, OH: Magee Brothers Publishing, 1916.

Robinson, George K. *History of Greene County, Ohio*. Chicago: S.J. Clarke Publishing, 1902.

Robinson, Marsha R., ed. *Purgatory between Kentucky and Canada: African Americans in Ohio*. Newcastle, UK: Cambridge Scholars Publishing, 2013.

Rowe, Jill E. *Invisible in Plain Sight*. New York: Peter Lang Publishing, 2017.

Royer, Donald M. *The Longtown Settlement, Darke County, Ohio: The History of a People from Slavery to Freedom and Independence*. Richmond, IN: self-published, 2003.

Salafia, Matthew. *Slavery's Borderland: Freedom and Bondage along the Ohio River*. Philadelphia: University of Pennsylvania Press, 2013.

Schwarz, Philip J. *Migrants Against Slavery: Virginians and the Nation*. Charlottesville: University Press of Virginia, 2001.

Schweninger, Loren. *Black Property Owners in the South, 1790–1915*. Urbana: University of Illinois Press, 1997.

Scott, Daniel. *A History of the Early Settlement of Highland County, Ohio*. Hillsboro, OH: Hillsborough Gazette, 1890.

Scranton, S.S. *History of Mercer County, Ohio*. Chicago: Biographical Publishing, 1907.

Shreve, Benford T. *Poems of Elizabeth Shreve-Chambers: Sketches of Her Life and Reminiscences*. Bayard, OH: Bradshaw Printing, 1919.

Simmons, William J. *Men of Mark: Eminent, Progressive and Rising*. Cleveland, OH: George M. Rewell & Company, 1887.

Stockard, Sallie Walker. *The History of Guilford County, North Carolina*. Knoxville, TN: Gault-Ogden Company, 1902.

Sutherland, Jonathan D. *African Americans at War: And Encyclopedia*. Santa Barbara, CA: ABC-CLIO, 2004.

Tucker, E. *History of Randolph County, Indiana*. Chicago: A.L. Kingman, 1882.

Turpin, Joan. *Register of Black, Mulatto and Poor Families in Four Ohio Counties, 1791–1861*. Bowie, MD: Heritage Books, 1985.

Washington, Booker T. *The Story of the Negro: The Rise of the Race from Slavery*. New York: Doubleday, Page & Company, 1909.

Willard, Eugene B., ed. *Standard History of the Hanging Rock Region of Ohio*. N.p.: Lewis Publishing Company, 1916.

Wilson, Frazer E. *History of Darke County, Ohio*. Milford, OH: Hobart Publishing, 1914.

Wilson, Stella Harger, and R.N. Nelson. *Centennial History of Rumley, Ohio, 1937–1937*. Self-published, 1937.

Wolfe, William G. *Stories of Guernsey County: History of an Average Ohio County*. Cambridge, OH: self-published, 1943.

Articles and Other

Advocate (Buffalo, NY). October 30, 1856.

African American Lives. "Who Am I? A Genealogy Guide." Thirteen, Media with Impact, www.thirteen.org.

AfriGeneas. "AfriGeneas Genealogy and History Forum Archive 2." www.afrigeneas.com.

Albrecht, Robert. "Neighborhood Not What It Used to Be—Black Enclave Gives Way to New Influx." *Columbus (OH) Dispatch*, May 14, 1996.

Allen, Nimrod B. "He Built His Own Resort." *Opportunity: Journal of Negro Life* 17, no. 4 (April 1939).

Antipodean. "Distributed A/C Book for William Ragland's Negroes." www.antipodean.com.

Anti-Slavery Bugle (Lisbon, OH). "Correspondence of the Morning Herald." August 21, 1846.

———. "Manumission of Slaves." April 28, 1848.

———. "Mercer County, Ohio." November 6, 1846.

ArcGIS Online. "Tracking Freedom: Tracing the Origins of Ohio's Free Blacks from 1803–1863." www.arcgis.com.

Barnesville (OH) Enterprise. "Captina African Methodist Episcopal Church Cemetery Restoration Remembered during Black History." February 22, 2017.

Baxter, Joan. "Godfrey Brown Builds a Church." *Xenia (OH) Daily Gazette*, February 16. 2019.

Black/Land Project. "When Place Makes Race." www.blacklandproject.org.

Brown, Mary Ann. "Vanished Black Rural Communities in Western Ohio." *Perspectives in Vernacular Architecture* 1 (1982).

Browning, Mary. "G.C. Mendenhall Had Slaves Taken to Ohio to Be Freed." *News & Record* (Greensboro, NC), November 27, 2013.

Buffalo (NY) Commercial. "Address by James L. Barton." March 1, 1848

Burke, Henry Robert. "Slavery in the Ohio River Valley." Lest We Forget, http://lestweforget.hamptonu.edu.

Cadiz (OH) Democratic Sentinel. "Prefer Slavery." Mary 28, 1857.

Campbell, Karen S. "Captain Ordinatus Simon Bolivar Wall." Let the Journeys Begin, https://letthejourneysbegin.wordpress.com.

Charlotte (NC) Democrat. "Liberation of Slaves." July 7, 1857.

———. "An Unkind Master." July 7, 1857.

Chicago Daily Tribune. "The Copperhead Church Movement." March 27, 1864.

Cincinnati (OH) Enquirer. "Charles Hammond on Free Negroes." April 5, 1865.

———. "Correspondence." August 6, 1852.

Cincinnati Journal of Homoeopathy 1, no. 6. (August 1851).

Colored Conventions. http://coloredconventions.org.

Daily Union (Washington, D.C.). "The Randolph Slaves." July 17, 1846.

Dayton (OH) Daily News. "Only a Very Few of Them Now Living." January 18, 1913.

Defrank, Robert A. *Times Leader* (Martins Ferry, OH). February 25, 2018.

DuBois, W.E.B. "Long in Darke." *Colored American Magazine* 17 (November 1909).

Encyclopædia Britannica editors. "Philipp Emanuel von Fellenberg." www.britannica.com.

Ervin, Bob. "Memories of Big Rock Shared." *Pike County (OH) News Watchman*, January 2, 2014.

Evening Star (Washington, D.C.). "A Black Watering Place." August 14, 1854.

Federal Writers' Project. "Slave Narratives: A Folk History of Slavery in the United States from Interviews with Former Slaves." https://memory.loc.gov/mss/mesn/120/120.pdf.

Feight, Andrew, "'Black Friday': Enforcing Ohio's 'Black Laws' in Portsmouth, Ohio." Scioto Historical, https://sciotohistorical.org.

Find A Grave. "William Harvey Brown." www.findagrave.com.

Free African Americans. "Virginia Slaves Freed After 1782." www.freeafricanamericans.com.

Galbreath, C.B. "Anti-Slavery Movement in Columbiana County." *Ohio Archaeological and Historical Quarterly* 30, no. 4 (October 1921).

Gallia (OH) Herald. "Lambert Land—A Lesson in History." November 3, 2013.

Gannon, Megan. "Race Is a Social Construct, Scientists Argue." *Scientific American*, February 15, 2016. www.scientificamerican.com.

GENi. "Abraham Van Meter: Will." www.geni.com.

Gray, Beverly J. "The Barnett Cemetery." www.angelfire.com/oh/chillicothe/ugrr.html. Accessed February 6, 2019.

———. "The Eden Baptist Church." www.angelfire.com/oh/chillicothe/ugrr. html. Accessed February 6, 2019.

Green County, Ohio. "Deed Volume 32 page 188." https://co.greene.oh.us.

Hancks, Larry. "The Emigrant Tribes: Wyandot, Delaware & Shawnee." Wyandot Nation of Kansas. www.wyandot.org.

Hannah, Jim. "Vanishing Act." *Wright State University Magazine* (Spring 2016). http://webapp2.wright.edu.

Heise, Robin. "From Mississippi to Greene County Ohio: The Journey of a Former Slave and Her Family." Yellow Springs Heritage, https://ysheritage.org.

Highland (County, OH) Weekly News. "The Colored Farmers in Ohio." August 2, 1867, 2.

———. "The Colored Farmers of Ohio." August 22, 1867.

History of American Women. "Sarah Jane Woodson Early." www.womenhistoryblog.com.

Homepage of James W. Loewen. "Showing Waverly in OH." https://sundown.tougaloo.edu.

Honeyman, Gale. "The Hanktown Community." Troy Historical Society, www.thetroyhistoricalsociety.org.

Hunt, W.M. "History of 'Africa.'" Wilbur H. Siebert Underground Railroad Collection, http://ohiomemory.org/cdm/search/collection/siebert.

Hunter, W.H. "The Pathfinders of Jefferson County." *Ohio Archaeological and Historical Publications* 6 (1898).

Ironton (OH) Register. "The Division of Property of the Emancipated Slaves of James Twyman." September 22, 1870.

———. "A Sudden Death." October 11, 1888.

Jackson (OH) Standard. "Editors." February 9, 1855.

———. "Notice." September 6, 1866.

———. "One Hundred and Ten!" February 17, 1887.

Jefferson's Monticello, www.monticello.org.

Johnson, Jim. "Shelby County's Black History Rooted in Virginia." *Shelby County (OH) News*, February 10, 2012.

J. Willard Marriott Library, University of Utah. "Hood, Frances Ann Stewart." Century of Black Mormons, https://exhibits.lib.utah.edu.

Lexington Township, Stark County, Ohio. "History of Lexington Township." http://lexingtontwpstarkco.com.

Liberator (Boston, MA). "A Colored Settlement." January 1, 1841.

———. "Essex County A.S. Society." July 10, 1840.

Library of Virginia, Virginia Memory. "John Warwick." Unknown Not Longer, https://unknownnolonger.virginiahistory.org.

Love, Edgar F. "Registration of Free Blacks in Ohio: The Slaves of George C. Mendenhall." *Journal of Negro History* 69, no. 1 (Winter 1984).

Lytle, Sharon L. "The Alston Freed Slaves." Peter Kivett Family Association, http://pkivfa.org.

Malloy, David E. "Man Says Church in Lawrence Was Underground Railroad Stop." *Herald-Dispatch* (Huntington, WV), July 13, 2016.

————. "Students Tell Blackfork Story." *Herald-Dispatch* (Huntington, WV), May 30, 2008.

Massie, Jim. "Payne Cemetery—Genealogical Group Hopes to Link Generations, Heritage to Black Burial Site." *Columbus (OH) Dispatch*, February 1, 1994.

————. "Riddles of the Past—More Mysteries Remain Buried Beneath Headstones at Payne Cemetery." *Columbus (OH) Dispatch*, June 10, 1994.

Maumee (OH) City Express. "Self Defence." June 8, 1839.

McRae, Bennie, Jr. "Bass and Clemens Cemeteries in Darke County, Ohio." Lest We Forget, http://lestweforget.hamptonu.edu.

"Narrative of David Barrett." *Anti-Slavery Record* 3, no. 7 (July 1837).

National Park Service. "James & Sophia Clemens Farmstead." Aboard the Underground Railroad, www.nps.gov.

NCpedia. "Newlin, John." www.ncpedia.org.

New York Tribune. July 12, 1851.

"Noah Spears." *Independent Monthly* 1, no. 3 (March 1869).

Ohio History Central. "Eden Baptist Church." www.ohiohistorycentral.org.

Ohio History Connection. "Settling Rossville." www.ohiohistory.org.

Ohio Memory. "Gabe N. Johnson's interview, Sept. 30, 1894." Wilbur H. Siebert Underground Railroad Collection. https://ohiomemory.org/digital/collection/siebert/id/6585/rec/4. Accessed February 14, 2019.

Ohio State Journal and Columbus (OH) Gazette. "Blacks and Mulattoes." May 3, 1827.

Olding, Mary Ann. "A Study of Ohio's Rural Settlements." *Cerebrum: Online Journal* 1, no. 1 (August 2017). www.grupoclifton.org.

Old Northwest Notebook. "The Unfinished Story of Negro Town." http://dpwilkens.blogspot.com.

Old Settlers Reunion. "The Old Settlers: A Nation Within Mecosta, Isabella & Montcalm Communities Including the Central Michigan Area." www.oldsettlersreunion.com.

Old Settlers Reunion Association. "Lett Families Settlement History & Genealogy." www.osra1977.org.

Patrick, Larry. "Street Signs Honoring History of Berlin Crossroads Going Up." Jackson County Chapter of the Ohio Genealogical Society, http://jacksoncountyohiogen.com.

Pike County (OH) Republican. "Life among the Lowly, No. 1." March 13, 1873.

————. "Life among the Lowly: Number II." November 20, 1873.

————. "Life among the Lowly, No. 3: Israel Jefferson: Recollections of a Monticello Slave." December 25, 1873.

Piqua (OH) Daily Call. "Blind Negro, Age 81, Tells Vividly of Early Slave Days." July 14, 1923.

————. "Former Slave of Randolph Dies in Piqua." December 22, 1903.

Pittsburgh Gazette. "A Colored Settlement." December 2, 1840.

————. "Slaves Emancipated." October 20, 1855.

Porcher, Connie. "Who Were the Randolph Slaves?" Miami County, Ohio, Genealogical Researchers. www.thetroyhistoricalsociety.org.

Portage (County, OH) Sentinel. "John Randolph's Slaves." December 9, 1846.

————. "Randolph's Slaves." August 12, 1846.

Portsmouth (OH) Daily Times. "Emancipation and Its Results." June 21, 1862.

Powell, C.A., B.T. Kavanaugh and David Christy. "Transplanting Free Negroes to Ohio from 1815 to 1858." *Journal of Negro History* 1, no. 3 (June 1916).

Price, Rita. "Memorial Honors Lambert Settlers." *Columbus (OH) Dispatch*, September 15, 2002.

Remarkable Ohio. "The Lambert Land Settlement." www.remarkableohio.org.

Richards, Laura. "The Gist Settlement." Washington Court House City Schools, www.wchcs.org.

Richmond (VA) Dispatch. "A Question of Color—Queer Case in Ohio." December 21, 1867.

Richmond (VA) Enquirer. "The Randolph Slaves." July 24, 1846.

Richwood (OH) Gazette. "Darke County." May 30, 1895.

Roberts, H.C. Interview by W.H. Siebert, July 5, 1895. https://ohiomemory.org/digital/collection/siebert/search

Robinson, Wilhelmina. "The Negro in the Village of Yellow Springs, Ohio." *Negro History Bulletin* 29 (1966).

"Roots and the New 'Faction.'" *The Virginia Magazine of History and Biography* 89, no. 1 (January 1981).

RootsWeb. "Brenda Keck Reed's Kith & Kin of VA, NC, TN, SC & Beyond." https://wc.rootsweb.com.

Ross, Donald, and Martha Breeden. "Freed Madison Slaves Leave Lasting Legacy." *Newsletter of the Madison County Historical Society*, May 2015.

Rowe, Jill E. "In Strength & Struggle: Free Black Communities in the Old Northwest." Paper presented at the Africa and the Atlantic World Conference, Kent State University, April 8, 2016.

————. "Mixing It Up: Early African American Settlements in Northwestern Ohio." *Journal of Black Studies* 39, no. 6 (July 2000).

Salem (OH) Daily News. "A Rich Colored Man Dead." May 12, 1894.

Schrader, Paul Mendel. "Historical Study of the Negro in Jackson Township, Pike County Ohio Located Just East of Waverly." *Waverly (OH) News*, July 1, 1959.

Setlock, Joelene McDonald. "Thomas Jefferson and Sally Hemings." Ohio University, www.ohio.edu

State of the Re:Union. "Pike County, OH: As Black as We Wish to Be." http://stateofthereunion.com.

Stevens, Joann. "The District's Woodson Family." *Washington Post*, December 1, 1977.

Thomas, Arthur L. "Where Are the Randolphs: A Surnaming Question." Presentation at the Ohio Academy of History–University of Dayton, April 9–10, 1999.

Times Recorder (Zanesville, OH). "Colored Citizens' News." September 25, 1925.

Triweekly Washington (D.C.) Sentinel. "Emancipation." October 13, 1855.

Turley, Alicestyne. "Spirited Away: Black Evangelicals and the Gospel of Freedom, 1790–1890." Dissertation, University of Kentucky, 2009.

Turner, Violet M. "Gist Settlement Keeps Alive Days of Long Ago." *Wilmington (OH) News-Journal*, July 25, 1936.

UNC Greensboro. "Petition 11483106 Details." Race & Slavery s Project, https://library.uncg.edu.

———. "Slave Ownership History for Estate of Worthington, Thomas." Race & Slavery Petitions Project, http://library.uncg.edu.

University of Washington School of Law. "Transcript: Q&A with Henry Louis Gates, Jr." www.law.washington.edu.

Vega, Teresa. "Part III: The DNA Trail from Madagascar to Virginia." Radiant Roots, Boricua Branches, http://radiantrootsboricuabranches.com/category/sylvia-ragland.

Vermont Telegraph. "Slaves Emancipated!" June 10, 1840.

Waldron, Bob. "Lambert Lands…Settlement for Slaves." *Columbus (OH) Dispatch*, December 15, 1963.

Welcome to the Lawrence County Register. "Poke Patch History." www.lawrencecountyohio.com.

Williams, Kevin. "Slavery's Long Legacy in a Corner of Ohio." Aljazeera America, October 5, 2015. http://america.aljazeera.com.

Wilson, John G. "Old Times: The Exodus of the 37 Blacks from Va. to Burlington in 1849." *Ironton (OH) Register*, March 5, 1896.

Woodson, Carter G., ed. *Journal of Negro History.* 5, no. 4. (1920).

Wright, Richard R., Jr. "Negro Rural Communities in Indiana." *Southern Workman* 37, no. 3 (March 1908).

Wyandotte (KS) Gazette. "John Randolph's Slaves." June 21, 1878.

Xenia (OH) Daily Gazette. "Freed Negroes of Early Days." February 6, 1936.

Xenia (OH) Daily News, July 30, 1900.

Yellow Springs News. "William Mills—'The Yellow Springs Man.'" March 25, 2010.

INDEX

W

ABOUT THE AUTHORS

A graduate of Miami and Ohio State Universities, David Meyers has written a number of local histories, as well as several novels and works for the stage. He was recently inducted into the Ohio Senior Citizens Hall of Fame for his contributions to local history.

Elise Meyers Walker is a graduate of Hofstra University and Ohio University. She has collaborated with her father on a dozen local histories, including *Ohio's Black Hand Syndicate* and *Lynching and Mob Violence in Ohio*. They are both available for presentations.

The authors' website is www.explodingstove.com, or follow them on Twitter and Instagram @explodingstove

Visit us at
www.historypress.com